Everyone's a

Games, simulations,
for exploring the Bible

by JIM BELBEN and TREVOR COOPER

A Bible Society Creative Handbook

For churches, teachers, and youth leaders

BIBLE SOCIETY

Stonehill Green, Westlea, Swindon SN5 7DG, England

© Bible Society and Trevor Cooper 1987

Unless otherwise stated, quotations from the Bible are from the Good News
Bible, published by the Bible Societies/Collins, © American Bible Society,
New York, 1966, 1971, 1976.

First published 1987

British Library Cataloguing in Publication Data
Belben, Jim
Everyone's a winner : games, simulations
and role plays to explore the Bible. ——
(A Bible Society creative handbook).
1. Bible——Study   2. Bible games and
puzzles   3. Games in Christian education
I.Title   II.Cooper, Trevor   III.Bible
Society
220' .07   GV1507.B5
ISBN 0–564–07782–8

Printed in Great Britain by Stanley L. Hunt (Printers) Ltd, Midland Road, Rushden,
Northants.

Bible Societies exist to provide resources for Bible distribution and use.
Bible Society in England and Wales (BFBS) is a member of the United Bible
Societies, an international partnership working in over 180 countries. Their
common aim is to reach all people with the Bible, or some part of it, in a
language they can understand and at a price they can afford. Parts of the
Bible have now been translated into approximately 1,800 languages. Bible
Societies aim to help every church at every point where it uses the Bible. You
are invited to share in this work by your prayers and gifts. Bible Society in
your country will be very happy to provide details of its activity.

Thanks

If there was room on this page to thank everyone who has had a hand in creating the activities in this book we would do so. But there isn't.

Literally hundreds of teenagers, youth workers, friends, colleagues, and researchers have at some stage or other offered a comment, asked a question, or had an idea which has affected the content of this book.

So instead of a long list of names we'd like to say a simple but deeply felt thank you to all those youth fellowships from Plymouth to Pitlochry and Dublin to Dover who let us use them as guinea pigs. Thanks for being so trusting and so adventurous.

And to all those in the later stages who have commented on the manuscript and the games themselves — thanks for both your encouragements and your criticisms.

Without your help this book would still be just a list of bright ideas. For better or worse you have helped make it happen. We hope you like the results, and we pray that these activities will bring an exciting variety to the Bible study programme of all who use them.

JIM BELBEN AND TREVOR COOPER

Foreword

Most of us see "games" as something rather frivolous. The word conjures up images of endless Scrabble sessions on Boxing Day, or table tennis tournaments down at the youth club. Something quite trivial.

And when people begin to take games too seriously — asking to have their ashes sprinkled on the local football club's pitch, or committing suicide when their team loses a vital match — we grow wary. "It's only a game, after all", we protest.

Only a game? For these reasons the church has never looked seriously at the potential of games as an educational medium. Yet in top-level management training, or military programmes, games are a highly-prized, indispensable part of effective teaching. Are we missing something?

I think we are. And so I warmly welcome this valuable book, in which Jim Belben and Trevor Cooper not only argue the case for games forcefully and clearly, but also supply a selection of some of the best — tried, tested, and guaranteed. And if your view of "education", deep down, is that *real learning* has less to do with "activities", "experiences", and "insights" than with stuffing your head with data and concepts — then it's worth reflecting that your ideas probably derive more from the ancient Greeks than from the Bible!

Greek thought had a lot to do with shaping our Western educational system. And, says Dr. Robert Ferris, "the Greek view leads toward isolation of the academy from the world, whereas the biblical view recognizes the world as our classroom. . . Educational systems rooted in the Greek view are characterized by *a drive to know*; those grounded in the Bible seek not only to know, but also *to do* and *to be*."

Doing things practically, trying them out, learning from experience, encountering what-would-you-do-if situations. . .these are all part of the biblical pattern of learning, as this book makes clear. Take it seriously. It *isn't* frivolous, even if it's fun. It will lead you and your group into unexpected, valuable discoveries about the Bible which you'd never gain in any other way!

John Allan

Youth evangelist and
"Greenbelt" speaker

Contents

	Page
Introduction	1
How to use this book	3
WHY PLAY GAMES?	4
What is a game?	4
Isn't Bible study better than games?	6
HOW TO PLAY GAMES	11
Which game, when?	11
Playing a game	14
Warming up	17
Debriefing	20
SECTION A THE BIBLE	27
1. Little Bible	
– barter to create the most useful abridged Bible	28
2. Connections	
– trace the threads linking the Old and New Testaments	32
3. DIY Bible	
– spend a whole weekend creating your own "manual of the church"	37
4. Best seller	
– create a cover for the Bible, to appeal to various audiences	49
5. Mix'n'match	
– test your comprehension of a passage by reconstructing it	54
6. Give us a proverb	
– look at the practical wisdom of Proverbs, and create modern proverbs on various themes	57

Page

SECTION B   THE CHRISTIAN COMMUNITY   65

7. Matching game
   – discover some of the joys and sorrows of boy-girl
   relationships   66

8. Money, money, money
   – see how the Bible could guide you in some important
   decisions   77

9. Bits and pieces
   – create a meaningful sculpture from a pile of bricks   89

10. One-hundred-thousand pounds
    – decide how your church should spend a vast legacy   95

11. Roll out the barrel
    – role-play the various members of a church who must
    decide on an important issue of Christian behaviour   101

12. Zac's map
    – create an itinerary for the walkabout of a visiting
    religious dignitary   122

13. First things first
    – do something about the great shortage of Bibles
    around the world   126

DESIGNING YOUR OWN GAMES
    – a conversation   138

CONCLUSION

RESOURCES   145

Index/table showing – suitability for your group
                    – preparation time
                    – playing time   147

Resources for games   148

Index of Bible references   149

General Index   151

Introduction

In a teaching experiment a few years ago a certain school was split in two. Half of the pupils were taught some geography by conventional means — a teacher up-front telling them fascinating facts, and every now and then giving them project work to do. The other half were taught the same geography by means of a simulation game.

At the end of the term, both groups were given the same "test" on what they had learned.

On average the group taught by conventional means were scoring 25 or 30% *higher* than the group taught by the simulation.

After a four-week break over the Easter holidays, both groups sat the *same* test at the beginning of the Summer term. Now, on average, the group taught by conventional means were scoring just 5 or 10% better than the others.

Finally, ten weeks later, at the end of the Summer term, after all the rush and panic of exams etc., both groups sat the *same* test again.

Now the group taught by the simulation were scoring on average 25% *more* than the group taught by conventional means.

The moral of that story is obvious. If you want to cram your class for a test they are sitting tomorrow, don't try a simulation. But if you are more interested in long-term effects, and your main aim is to help the pupils understand a subject, use a simulation.

Everyone's a winner. The pupils learn better. The teacher teaches better.

Simulations take a long time to invent, to test, and a long time to prepare and play, but it is worth the investment of time and energy if you believe, as we do, that it is the long-term results that really matter.

Christian growth, after all, continues over a life-time. It's not something that is "achieved" in a few days, months, or even years. How many of our rushed youth group sessions seemed great fun at the time and caused quite a buzz, but a fortnight later seemed totally unmemorable? We believe that the games in this book will repay the time and effort you give to them because they live on, long after they're played.

And not just youth groups — but adult groups, house groups, leadership groups, and any training group — can discover how games can help us learn from one another and from our own experience.

There's a second reason that everyone's a winner. In our society people compete. They compete for jobs, for grants, to be top of the league or the ladder. Nations compete to be the richest, the best armed, or the biggest. There is an obvious need for activities that reinforce the opposite values of cooperation. That help people help others to learn. That spread skills around instead of concentrating them in one selected individual.

True, there's quite a lot of competition in this book. Most games need a bit. But there are no losers. Only learners. And if everyone learns, then everyone wins.

In this book you will find thirteen games, role-plays, and simulations to help your church or youth group explore the teaching of the Bible on a variety of subjects.

These are all proven activities — we could have written a much longer book if we'd included the ones that *almost* worked! The games help the players to look beyond the printed pages of the Bible to the principles and issues that it contains.

Not that the word "game" appears anywhere in the Bible. Nor, for that matter, will you find role-play mentioned, or simulation. So, as so often when the Bible has nothing direct to say on a subject, we've thought carefully about the arguments for the use of games in churches. We've come to believe that not only do they work (that is quite clear), but that in many ways they copy the Bible's own method of teaching, through imagination and experience.

Along with the games, then, in this book you'll find a number of short chapters on such knotty problems as "Why play games at all?" and "Isn't Bible study better than games?" If your primary requirement in reading this book is to think through the theory then you will need to read these chapters first.

We think, though, that many people already believe in using games and will have discovered how easily they can release the imagination, and teach by direct experience. Perhaps you have already discovered why games are such an ideal learning method:

■ Everyone gets involved in the game — there are no spectators

■ A game is an active process, which means that what is learnt will be better remembered

■ A well-designed game will usually cope with a very wide range of ability and knowledge, giving something to everybody

■ Players control their own participation and are not being forced, so they are more willing to give their full attention; there is the added advantage in religious circles that the game is not usually threatening to the uncommitted person

We have found games work well to raise issues and explore attitudes, but above all to bring the Bible closer to our own world. To hear it more clearly. We hope you find the same.

How to use this book

. . . If you are in a tearing hurry to find a game

Go to the index on page 147. Choose a game that suits your group and doesn't take too long to prepare. Prepare it. Play it. Then come back and read the book properly.

. . . If you want to find out what games we've provided

Browse through the list of contents, which gives you a brief idea of each game. Then look at those games which take your fancy.

. . . If you want to choose a game for a particular group, purpose, length of time, or Bible passage

Use the indexes at the back of the book.

. . . If you want to think about what you're doing

Read "Why play games?" and "How to play games", to help your thoughts along.

. . . If you want to make your own games

Good idea! Have a look at the final chapter on designing your own games.

Why play games?

What is a game?

Let's begin by deciding what we are talking about. What is a game?

Everyone agrees that snakes and ladders is a game. So is table tennis. What do they have in common?

First, it's obvious that people play them because *they are fun* or to put it another way, they are played for their own sake. You don't have to ask "What is the point of table tennis?" or claim that snakes and ladders is an educational experience. True, the participants put a lot of energy and concentration into playing them. And they may care if they win or they lose, particularly if there is a prize involved. But it's enough that they are fun. The players would not claim that the activity itself has any point, or gets them anywhere.

Second, the *result is unimportant*, which is one of the reasons why it is enjoyable. Real emotions, real concentration, and real energy can be used in a setting where the outcome doesn't matter. Steam can be let off easily. A game is no longer a game if the "wrong" result is going to have a disastrous effect on someone's life. Which is the biggest difference between the tearful tennis star on Wimbledon Centre Court, and the youth club member enjoying a fun game of table tennis.

Third, it is important that the *result of the game is not fixed beforehand*. In this sense it's like life. Anything can happen, and does! Even though one outcome is often a bit more likely than others.

Finally, all games have what game-makers call *internal logic*. This is not quite the same as saying they have rules. It's more a matter of saying that the rules fit together into a package which makes sense. Everyone knows the rules are artificial. Different rules could easily be invented. Yet players accept them because the game is seen as a little universe on its own, with its own laws of behaviour, and there is not too much worry about how realistic they are. But if the rules are not logical — for instance if you design a game in which the aim is to collect money, then add a rule which penalizes you if you do — the game will fall apart.

So games:

■ Are involving, and are fun to play for their own sake

■ Do not have a lot depending on the outcome

■ Are not fixed

■ Do have "internal logic"

If people are to be fully involved, all these features are important.

When the rules of a game seem connected in some way with real life, then the game may be called a simulation — because it simulates real life. If the game has a lot to do with the way people behave, then it may be called a role-play.

That not only sorts out some definitions, but has also given us a good way into seeing why we play games at all, and how they can be useful. Players can learn:

- *Facts* which they need to learn in order to play the game
- *Insight* into the issues within a game
- *Evaluation* of decisions made within the game
- *A sense of priorities* and an appreciation of what happens when different groups have a different sense of priorities
- *Self-awareness* of how they played, what they felt, how they responded, what their attitude was
- About *consequences* of their actions, attitudes, and feelings

In practice any one game will tend to major on just one or two of the above areas of learning.

In addition, as we have already seen, games allow emotions to be set free in a controlled and safe setting. As a group leader you will immediately see the usefulness of the things above.

But let's be clear about one basic thing. All the results listed above are consequences, or may be even "side effects," of games. To succeed at all a game must first of all be fun to play for its own sake. At some level or other players *must* enjoy it. No one claims that the main point of table tennis is to improve hand/eye coordination, or that the point of Monopoly is to increase the players' envy or sympathy for landlords. These things might or might not follow, but they are not sufficient motivation to get players playing the game.

So although all the games in this book have a learning objective stated clearly, and although as the leader you can confidently expect your group to learn from this game a new fact, insight, or attitude, they are first of all, we believe, worth playing for their own sake. All are fun. All have uncertain outcomes, and all have a sensible internal logic. Without these we would be cheating you and the future players of the game. They would feel used, and would soon react by showing a distaste for game playing.

Having said that, an important "side-effect" we've looked for in these games is risk-free experience. Players can try out an attitude during a game. They can take it seriously, yet at the same time keep it isolated in the separate bubble-universe of the game. In this way players can explore "What if . . ."

What if I listened to the advice of friends and ignored what I believe the Bible teaches? Or what if my church suddenly had one-hundred-thousand pounds to spend? What if . . .

In some ways this method of trying on the mantle of experience is safer than the normal group discussion. In a discussion what can happen is that "the correct answer" will be effectively sold by the leadership. At the time it is accepted; but because there has been no mental or emotional run-through of these views, they are often dropped later. This is particularly true for the quieter members of a group, who don't even have the benefit of testing their ideas by presenting them verbally.

Games, however, provide a natural testing ground for attitudes. Those attitudes that can't stand the game will certainly not stand up to real life.

Yet some of you might still say "Isn't Bible study better than games?" That's such an important subject that it needs a heading of its own . . .

Isn't Bible study better than games?

Please read this, particularly if you feel that playing table tennis is one thing but using games to explore the Bible is another.

There are probably two reasons for thinking this.

First of all, games might seem to you to be too flippant for this sort of job. But think again. It probably won't worry you that games are too much *fun*. Things that are fun help us learn. After all, isn't it the school lessons that were fun that we remember best? But at the same time as being fun, their aim was serious. And everyone taking part knew that. No, it's not that games are fun that is the problem — it's just that if a group of people are willing to spend time learning from the Bible, doesn't "fooling around" with games give entirely the wrong sort of message? We disagree, and in a moment we'll explain our reasons.

Second, you may feel that games are simply *no good* for the job of explaining and unravelling the important yet complex teaching of the Bible. Take, for example, what Paul had to say about the importance of the resurrection, when he wrote for the first time to the church based in Corinth (1 Corinthians 15.1–58 if you want to look it up). What game could possibly take people through Paul's thinking in an affirmative and logical way?

In short, isn't a group Bible study better than a game? And the answer is yes, sometimes. But no, not always.

Group Bible study is an extremely effective way of doing certain things. It is a good way to study hard-to-understand passages, to learn "doctrines", to see inter-connections between different parts of the Bible. So this *would* probably be the right way to look at Paul's teaching about the resurrection. But many parts of the Bible do not teach by logic. They do not argue "If this, then this, and therefore that".

This can hardly be a surprise. God has never claimed to speak in a series of interrelated logical propositions. Our faith is founded on his actions in the history of a nation, and the history of a Man. The Bible records God's actions in these events, and explains his intentions.

The Bible never starts any chapter with the words "this is the whole truth about God, summarized". Instead, it teaches in small doses. Each story has a different theme and different emphasis. The key truths appear again and again, but to get the full picture you need all the stories. And not just the stories, but the prophecies, reflections, and meditations.

So we can learn something about God from Job's suffering — but not everything. And the vengeance of God in "the pillar of salt" (Genesis 19) does not contradict the mercy of God when the fish spewed up Jonah. Through many hints, experiences, puzzles, stories, wonders, and not a little common sense, we learn about the Creator of the universe.

We need all this, because it is in exactly this fuzzy, wandering way that we begin to see the pattern God has in mind for our own lives. Christians are guided not only by the logic of doctrine but by their day-to-day experience of God.

So we need the whole Bible. We need the arguments, the precision, the facts, and the doctrines. Without these how would we think? But we also need the allegories and mysteries, the stories, the sense of wonder. We need something larger than a set of equations. Without this our faith is unfeeling, mechanical. When God wanted to tell the world what he was like he didn't send a letter or a thesis, he sent Jesus, so people could live with him, hear him, talk with him, and feel his power.

And within the Bible itself we see the principles of learning through *role-play*, *case-study*, *activity*, and *experience*, as an important part of good communication.

Role-play in particular often makes an appearance. We don't mean here the acted parables of the prophets Ezekiel or Jeremiah, which are closer to illustrated sermons. Rather we would focus on the feasts and offerings of Israel which were elaborate, ritualized role-plays and which were clearly envisaged as teaching media. For example in Exodus 12.25–27 the Passover ritual is seen as having a learning objective for the young Israelites: "When you enter the land that the LORD has promised to give you, you must perform this ritual. When your children ask you, 'What does this ritual mean?' you will answer . . .''

And *case-study*? The prophet Nathan, sent to confront David with the enormity of his sin against Uriah and Bathsheba, produced his effect by inviting David to imagine himself in a fictional situation first, "What would you do, David, if . . .'' (2 Samuel 12.1–15).

Jesus, who used so many different methods to teach his disciples, invited them to learn through *activity* and *experience*. He sent them off to find coins in the mouths of fish (Matthew 17.27), or to sink their nets where there shouldn't have been a catch (John 21. 6) — activities which had meaning far beyond their immediate application. By doing them the disciples would grasp some new understanding of Jesus.

Even more important, when the time came for the disciples to continue Jesus' healing and teaching ministry, he sent them out two by two to try it for themselves and to come back and report on what happened (Luke 10.1–20).

Jesus understood what many of us today feel so strongly — that learning through doing, through playing, through feeling, and through sharing is as important as learning through hearing.

Now we can see why games might have a part to play. Games appeal to the many parts of our nature, not just the logical. The right game at the right time can get through where a discussion might not. From the many observations and insights within the game, we add to our knowledge of God.

Let's take an example from this book. In "DIY Bible" participants share their experiences of the church. They express them in songs, poems, letters, rules, and stories. Over the course of a weekend the church is looked at from all angles.

Towards the end of the game, the participants begin to see that some viewpoints are more useful than others. That some statements about the church have more permanence. That some explanations help them understand it that much better.

The effect is that of a kitchen cupboard spilled open. Out has come everything, from the baked beans to the rolling pin. Gradually you sort through the mess on the floor until finally you are left with what you need to make your meal.

What the participants discover in this game is the variety in the church. The complexity of Christian experience. As they turn again to the writings of Paul concerning the church they see greater meaning in his instruction to the Corinthians or the Philippians, whose experiences and whose problems were as varied as theirs.

The point of this book, then, is not to "replace" group Bible study, but to be a useful addition.

There is another point, however, possibly more important still. Everyone knows that teaching in the Bible always occurs to meet a need, and not in a vacuum. Paul wrote to small groups of worried Christians. Jesus responded to some of the burning questions of his disciples. The prophets spoke out against the excesses of their time. They taught to meet a need. In the same way, our "teaching" should aim to meet a need. Our Bible study should never be in a vacuum. Everyone knows this as well, but it can still be difficult.

Games can help here because they raise issues without presupposing answers. For example, one of the games in this book raises the issue of boy/girl relationships. It is called "Matching game". Whenever the issue of dating is discussed in a youth group you quickly hit the problem that people cannot agree what the questions are that need answering. So the function of this game is simply to get some agreement on what issues are central, and what questions the group think it important to discuss. And if the game goes well it will nearly always generate a real interest in the answers.

This means that, in a way, games are serious. They are *not* flippant, and they *don't* give the wrong impression about the importance of what is being done. In fact it is the opposite.

All the same, the Bible can pose problems for anyone designing games. Let's look at why this is.

The subjects that lend themselves well to games are ones that are:

1. Open-ended — i.e. where the outcome is uncertain and doesn't really matter.

2. Part of day to day life now.

3. Where the amount of information to be mastered prior to playing the game is minimal.

4. Where people feel free to try out openly attitudes and opinions that are not their own, and which might be considered unacceptable outside the game world.

Now consider the Bible:

1. In many cases the Bible is closed data. The Bible has already stated its opinion on issues, and we either agree or disagree with it. But we are not going to be able to change it.

2. Very few people, even very few Christians, actually spend much time with the Bible from day to day. Add to which the fact that even the most recent stories happened about 2,000 years ago.

3. To get a true biblical picture on a subject you must sometimes read hundreds of verses, or even chapters, scattered around a vast book.

4. People may feel scared of disagreeing with the Bible, or with what they have been told the Bible says. Even within a game they will not enter into a debate with it.

So if we are to use the Bible effectively in games we must generally concentrate on particular functions of the Bible.

In this book, then, you will find games which:

1. Explore how we feel *about the Bible*. "Little Bible" is one such. It uses our own knowledge of the Bible, our favourite and less favourite books, to explore the Bible as a whole.

2. Pin-point a subject prior to *Bible study*. "Matching game" is an issue-raising game. It allows the Bible to be read with more interest because the game has raised some questions on which the Bible can speak.

3. Simulate situations in which *we try to act biblically*. "Zac's map" does this. Having laid down a biblical precedent we attempt to follow that precedent. And we discover how difficult it sometimes is.

4. Teach about the *nature of the Bible itself*. "DIY Bible" traces the process by which we got our Bible. As a result we can approach it both as God's word, and yet the product of some very varied human experiences.

5. Investigate the ways *people use the Bible*. To be honest, we all know there are good and bad ways to use it. In "Roll out the barrel" we see the contrast between the use of dubious biblical precedents, and more considered biblical judgements.

6. Help us *value our own bibles more*. "First things first" demonstrates the need around the world for this book that we tend to take so much for granted.

The above has tried to make you enthusiastic about games from the theoretical point of view. We must be mad! No doubt about it, the most convincing argument is to try it out, and play a game. And we hope that is what you will soon be doing. So let's move on to How to play games.

How to play games

Which game, when?

Games do need to be chosen carefully. You are responsible for your group and their learning, and you must not only choose a game which suits them and their needs, but also play it at the best time.

This is something which we have learnt the hard way, and we'd like to help you avoid repeating our mistakes.

Obviously you will be looking for a game that:

- Has aims that you share
- Is suitable for your age-group
- Will fit the time available

So at the end of the introduction to each game you will find the information you need to make those choices.

In addition, the indexes give you many ways of finding suitable games.

But none of these are hard and fast rules. Other factors will influence your choice.

Your programme

Are you looking for an introduction to a topic? Or a summing up? Or perhaps you are at mid-point, wanting to revive interest?

Some games are best played cold, but some benefit from a bit of prior discussion of the subject.

The mood of the group

Some games work best when a group is relaxed. Other games are very good at warming a group up. So, think how well the group know each other. This is perhaps particularly important with older groups, especially when the members might have "appearances" to keep up.

Then again, if the group are likely to be bouncy, or serious, tense, or flippant, choose a game to meet their mood — and perhaps transform it, if that's what you want. "Bits and pieces", for example, is a physical game with a lot of moving about, as is "Connections". "Best seller" and "Money, money, money" are quieter and more sedate.

Their knowledge

You will need to think about the level of knowledge needed for the game. None of the games in this book need profound knowledge of the Bible, but in some of them a little background will help. Does your group know enough to play the game?

Their maturity

How mature are the players? If powerful feelings are evoked in the game it can be less than useful to play it with a group who are simply not ready to handle those emotions seriously. "Matching game" is one such.

Context

Remember, too, that many games leave people on a high. So if you plan to use one at the end of a weekend or day conference, make sure that there is a chance to wind down afterwards. And think ahead to check that the players won't be too tired. Games require concentration and no one gets much satisfaction from struggling to do well when they're fighting heavy eyes.

Attitudes

Think, too, whether the subject of the game is one on which the group already hold fixed views. Are their views informed or biased? A game can make them question those views, and break down prejudice. For example "Roll out the barrel" seems to be extremely effective at bringing out and challenging views on the subject of alcohol.

Interest

On the other hand, if the group have no interest at all in the topic then you want a game which will stir up interest. "First things first" is an example of such a game.

All this probably sounds obvious. In fact, it is obvious. But that didn't stop us making mistakes. For example, Trevor used "Roll out the barrel" at the end of a day conference, allowing no time for a proper debrief. Result — frustration at having no time to talk out the issues raised.

Jim tried "Money, money, money" with a group who'd already done a lot of work on the subject. Result — disinterest. They thought they'd got beyond that point.

Trevor used "Matching game" with a group which currently had tensions relating to romantic relationships — and the game made them worse!

Jim tried an early version of "Bits and pieces" with a group who hardly knew each other, and which contained at least one awesome "authority" figure. The game spluttered its way to a halt!

So, please think through the points we've made in this chapter, and so minimize the mistakes.

Generally . . .

First, avoid the temptation always to use games as fillers, when you can't think of anything else to do. If you do this you'll soon find the group have realized what is going on, and will start to feel manipulated.

Second, don't go overboard, and start piling the games on top of each other. They are a unique learning tool, but they work best when used sparingly. So use creative work on a topic — poems, posters, plays, stories, and songs. Use discussion. Use case-work. Use talks. Use games to provide the spark, to raise the questions, and to break down prejudices, or indifference.

Third, many of these games grew out of our church youth work. So we might give the impression in this book, therefore, that games are only useful in youth work. That obviously isn't the case. The fact that games are used so widely in management training should indicate that there is a great potential for using games with adults.

Of course, adults may have a greater resistance to games. They may suspect you of wasting their time, or of trying to manipulate them. So go easy. But games such as "Little Bible", "Mix'n'match", "One-hundred -thousand pounds", "Bits and pieces", and "First things first", will all work very successfully with adult groups.

Wherever possible we have indicated in the "suitable for" box, and in the index, whether the game has yet been tried with adults.

Last, a word about timing. In deciding what game to use never miss out the question, "Have I got time to prepare it, play it, and debrief it?" Too many games are spoiled by the organizer underestimating the time necessary and finding themselves horribly rushed, or else taking a rash decision to try out their own half-hour adaptation of a two-hour game and being massively disappointed when it flops. Games really do take longer than other learning media. In fact it's almost a universal rule that they take longer than we expect. They cannot be shortened without crucial loss.

We are aware that most youth groups have a well-defined time slot to fill and some of these games may seem unrealistically long. But you are in control of your programme and a group is unlikely to resist a suggestion for a longer session than usual if they are convinced that the activity they are to try out is good fun and relevant.

Playing a game

These guidelines aim to help you ensure that any game you play is a success. It is based on our experience, including one or two disasters! Not that disasters are very common, because games are nearly unbreakable. Their big advantage is that the players all want to enjoy themselves, and all want the game to succeed. This makes them a much more reliable type of activity than, say, a discussion or a talk. Once you have chosen your game, what do you do next?

Preparation

It goes without saying that you should read through the whole game outline to start with. With the help of preparation notes under each game it is unlikely that you'll forget any of the implements you'll need. Also, look at the suggested variations to see if some are appropriate for your group. While on the subject, a word of explanation about "Variations" and "Other uses" — two headings you'll find in most game outlines. "Variations" suggests minor refinements that could add extra interest to this game for your group. "Other uses", on the other hand, suggests how you could substantially remodel the game for an entirely different purpose. But back to preparation. Many other things need forethought. We've already mentioned the emotional state of the gamesters. Will they be tired (for example at the end of a houseparty), shy, boisterous, or perhaps serious? It's important not only to choose the right game but to decide in advance how you will get the group's enthusiasm for it. And that means planning the warm-up. See page 17 for more on warming up.

Another thing that needs some careful thought beforehand is how you are going to explain the game. A garbled briefing is an effective way to ruin even the best game. We've learnt always to write out instructions more or less in full, except in the simplest cases. No doubt about it, this is boring. But it is worth it. That's why we've done it for you. Most games include a suggested briefing, presented in bold type.

Incidentally:

1. Insist on going through all instructions before taking questions. Otherwise you will find that the questions break the flow, and probably you would have covered the point anyway.

2. Make sure that your instructions don't give the impression that great cleverness or special knowledge is needed.

3. Try and give a feeling for how serious the game is.

Finally, you need to plan the debrief. As we have a whole section (page 20) on this most important subject, we won't take it any further now.

So in preparation, make sure you:

- Gather all the equipment you need
- Choose the right warm-ups
- Get the briefing right
- Plan the debriefing

Now you're ready to play the game.

Playing

After a good briefing things should run smoothly, but you will continue to have two roles, and how you exercise those is important. If you are a born autocrat or a busybody, restrain your natural desires and let the players get on with it. From now on you are referee and encourager.

Referee

Someone has to be referee, in one form or another. And that "one form or another" needs getting right. Pick an appropriate leadership style and stick to it.

For example, in "Roll out the barrel" one of us usually adopts the role of caretaker. Thus we can stay in character when we tell the group how much longer they have got, or that they're laughing too loud! The group easily accepts this.

In other role-playing games it seems more appropriate to stand on the sidelines, and interfere from there when necessary. Interference *will* be necessary sometimes, and expected by the game players. This is, after all, how many sports are played, with a judge or referee. For example, on odd occasions players will discover loopholes. If that happens, freeze everyone and publicly alter the rules to close the loophole.

Above all, remember that whenever you open your mouth and say something, you do, as it were, become part of the "process" the players are engaged in. Thus you will, like it or not, affect the dynamics of the game. So in general, interfere as little as possible. Certainly never try to manipulate the overall course of a game, even if it is taking the players off in quite unexpected directions.

Encourager

Sometimes your job includes encouragement or giving hints. For example, in "Little Bible", some groups are at first very unsure of themselves, particularly if they don't know much about the Bible. For us it is normal practice in this game, and others like it, to wander round reassuring the players and giving mild help where requested.

This has the added advantage of checking that they know what they're supposed to be doing. However well you've explained the rules, small doubts often arise when people are playing the game, usually because they've just realized how a particular rule is going to make life difficult for them, or sometimes because they've seen how they can use it to clobber another player.

Four stages in a game

You will usually find that games pass through four stages. It is useful to watch out for these, because they help you to call a halt at the right time, neither too early nor too late.

1. There is confusion and excitement. The players are trying to sort out how they will play the game. If they are in teams, they will be jostling for positions in the team. This is the time for wandering around unobtrusively and checking that rules are fully understood.

2. There will be determined, and well-directed, activity. At this stage strategies for playing the game start firming up. This is a good time for spotting any players who are liable to "drop out". They can be given the encouragement they need to continue.

3. For games with some competitive element there will be a third stage, of hectic activity, as the front-runners chase each other to the winning post. Those with no hope of winning will be fully engaged in loss-cutting, and may need encouraging. For other sorts of game this third stage can be created by setting a time-limit. For example, in "Connections", at the start, we give a rough idea of how long there is to play the game, and then at a given point, suddenly announce a deadline ten minutes away.

4. The fourth stage of a game is boredom. Don't let it get this far! It's always better to end too early than too late.

That's all there is to actually playing games. You now need to go on to read the guidelines on warming up and debriefing (pages 17 and 20). Then you're off on your travels around the book.

Warming up

If you have ever played games before you will know already how important it is to warm up. It makes all the difference between dull apathy and keen involvement. So never start a game without being sure that the group are at least a little in the mood. In adult groups the warm-up can be even more crucial — given the adults' healthy caution about "game-playing".

Groups usually find their own distinctive way of warming up. One we heard of would precede a game with a drama sketch on the subject. But, in our experience, most groups will use games to warm up — and many of you will have your own favourites. Use them. Donna Brandes' *Gamester's Handbooks* are excellent books, full of good ideas. Here are some more. We have put all the games together like this so you can easily pick and choose what you want. They are grouped under headings but they are in no way limited to that usage.

Names

In a newish group, and especially in an adult group, it is imperative that most people know most other people's names, otherwise communication is stunted. So games to learn names, to remind you of names, or to take away the guilt of having forgotten names, are essential.

Here are two.

Name-plus

Names are often forgotten because there is nothing special about them. You might meet one hundred Davids and forget each one, or call them all John. But meet one Sebastian or Myrtle, and they will stay in mind because the name itself is notable.

In this game, the idea is to think of something notable and memorable to attach with your totally unnotable and unmemorable name. For instance, I am Jim, and to make my name memorable as I say it I will kiss you on both cheeks, like a Russian diplomat. You must repeat this — i.e. say my name and kiss me on both cheeks!

Everybody prepares themselves in this way — name and memorable action — then as they circulate around the room, they introduce themselves, in their chosen way, to any whom they do not know.

Rhymes with a reason

We can remember names better if they are associated with another word with a similar sound. This game is a test of your poetic ability if your name is

Felicity or Ferdinand, but for most of us the act of putting our name into a two-line rhyme should not be too demanding.

For example, "I'm usually known as Patrick,
                     and I once scored a hat-trick."

As leader, you should write your own rhyme beforehand. Use the basic first line:

"I'm usually known as (insert your name — one, two, three and four syllable names will fit)".

And then write a second line, to rhyme. It doesn't need to be true!

Everyone makes up their own rhyme (they can completely change the form of the rhyme if they wish, as long as they include their name and a word to rhyme with it).

Then circulate around the room exchanging rhymes, and repeating the ones you hear. It makes it much easier to remember names, at the same time as exercising those forgotten word skills.

Move makers

These games are a cross between ice-breakers and physical warm-ups. They get the group concentrating on a single central task, and thus prepare the way for a game. They have little point in themselves, other than they are good fun and get people working together.

Geometry

Geometry at school was awful, but then they didn't teach it like this.

Split into smaller groups of three to five. Now, lying on the ground, use your bodies to make up specified geometrical shapes. For instance a square, a triangle, a cone, a straight line, a circle, a half-circle, a dotted line, a pyramid, a sphere (that's a very difficult one) etc. This also gets people into smaller groups and by using their bodies together, begins the process of working as a team.

Hot line

Everyone has a page of a newspaper. They must arrange themselves in line according to whose page has got the most, or least, of a specified subject — e.g., the person with the most pictures is at one end, the person with the least is at the other.

Follow this with more arrangements — the longest headline; the tallest headline; most articles; biggest page number; most recent date. They must rearrange themselves as a new line each time.

The fun (or chaos) starts when you introduce some subjective searches — e.g., the most boring sentence; the saddest story; the funniest cartoon.

This game, with its combination of physical movement, agreement, and comparisons, is an excellent ice-breaker.

All change

Everyone picks up an object. (Play this game in a room crowded with objects such as books, ornaments, knives, forks, cassettes, table-tennis bats, etc.) They must swap their object, on a given signal, for another object with the same number of letters, the same colour, something bigger, something smaller, something used for the same purpose, etc. — whatever the leader announces.

This encourages lateral thinking, as well as encouraging interaction and negotiating/bartering skills.

Weigh in

Bring your bathroom scales. Announce some random weight — e.g., 25 stone 13 lbs. The group must split into smaller groups that are as near this total weight as possible. Watch out for weight-sensitive people. Some anonymity is assured at the weigh-in if two or three people weigh themselves together — i.e., one person on another's back if necessary.

This can be a good way to get people into teams.

Instead of total weight, you could ask them to get into groups of a specified total height (bring a tape measure). You will quickly see how width of mouth or span from fingertip-to-fingertip could be used instead.

Arguments

Finally, a game that we find most versatile in helping prepare for role-plays, or any arguing/discussing game.

Get into pairs. Sit opposite your partner. Decide who is A and who is B. A chooses a particularly unusual, rare, or dangerous pet to keep — e.g. killer-whale, or a spiny ant-eater. B has one minute to dissuade A from choosing this course of action.

B then chooses a particularly dangerous and unusual hobby — e.g., collecting cruise missiles, or swimming the Pacific Ocean, and A has one minute to dissuade B from pursuing it.

Debriefing

This section deals with the subject of *debriefing*. This is the period immediately after the game when the players talk about the game, usually in a group discussion. It is an important subject, though debrief is an awful jargon word, and if you know a better one please tell us.

A lot of useful learning takes place at this stage. The players will want to talk about the game, and what happened to them. By listening to each other and describing their own experience they clarify what they have learnt.

It's impossible to say how much is learnt at this stage, compared with how much is learnt during the game itself. It's certainly a different type of learning. And it probably depends on the particular game. In "DIY Bible", a lot of insight seems to come while actually playing the game. In "Matching game" on the other hand, the players are so involved with point-scoring that it is not until the discussion afterwards that they discover what was happening to them during the game.

Some would say it is worth spending more time on the debrief than on the game itself. This is particularly important where deep emotions and feelings have been expressed.

Any game where the main aim is to explore and observe the way particular people behave can be traumatic affairs — many management games are like this. Our games, however, are on the whole a lot less threatening. But the debrief must always be long enough to allow the group to express what they feel about the game, and what they have learnt.

In the debrief as much as at any other time, you must use your instinct. Be sensitive to how much the group has to say. You will usually need to allow more time than you originally anticipated. Games usually overrun.

There are two basic debrief questions — "What happened?" and "What have I learned?". To save us repeating ourselves thirteen times over, through the book, we wish to suggest here some general guidelines on how to ask those questions, why they are important, and what to do if a debrief seems difficult.

Phase 1 – What happened?

Debrief questions must start off by being about the game itself. That is what the players will want to talk about. Let them talk about what happened on that occasion, *even if it wasn't quite what you expected or hoped*:

- Who won? Who lost? How did they feel?
- Who cheated? Who kept the rules? Why?
- Who enjoyed it? Who didn't? Why?
- What went wrong? Why?
- Who opted out? How did they feel?
- What was the best strategy for winning? The worst?

For certain games you will want to ask particular questions that concentrate on people's feelings as they played:

- Were they irritated?
- Did they feel boxed in?
- Did they have control over what was going on?
- Did they have a chance to persuade people to their point of view?

And so on.

These questions focus on facts and feelings. So they allow each person to air their opinions and experiences in a personal way. At this stage everyone is equal, because all have experienced the game.

If necessary take note of what people say, and refer back to it later in the discussion, but at this stage *do not try* to interpret what the game is about. Only after you've talked about this particular experience is it wise to start talking about what the game teaches.

This first phase should cover up to half of the debrief. When the discussion seems to be veering naturally towards interpretation, that is a signal to move to phase 2.

Phase 2 – What have we learned?

In some games, this will be pretty obvious. If so, the aim at this stage is simply to allow people to say in their own words what they have learned, and thus be able to reinforce it for themselves.

This phase of discussion should open with questions such as:

- What do you think the point of the game was?
- Have you come across this situation anywhere before?
- In what ways is the game like real life?

Each game includes specific questions to help in this aspect of debriefing.

We've worked hard on the debrief questions in this book. We've used them. They work. But they might not be the right ones for your group.

If you do need to invent your own debrief questions, remember it's important to keep them open-ended, and not let the question indicate that there is one, and only one, right answer. And don't keep coming back to a question until you get the answer you expected.

Let the views of the group emerge from their own experience of playing the game. Avoid *teaching*. You may have the authority, but now is not the time. Groups learn from games by shared experience. Let that experience flower — your wisdom is needed in the way you guide discussion, and lay emphasis.

This is not straightforward. It needs prior thought. But do be especially careful not to let all the previous times you have played this game intrude. Ignore the ghosts-of-games-past. Expect nothing, let this occasion and this discussion develop in its own way.

Now for some more general points concerning debriefing.

Coffee break

Immediately after a game it can be a good idea to serve coffee. This gives a quarter-of-an-hour for people to wind down after the game, if this is needed. During this time they will talk to each other about the game. This can be useful for learning, as it helps fix their minds on what has happened. It also means that they will have had a chance to tell *someone* the funny/ frustrating thing that happened to them in the game, or the marvellous coup they pulled off, and it is therefore less likely to make a time-consuming re-appearance during the discussion later.

Smaller groups

There is room for experiments with split debriefing, where the whole group is split into sub-groups, each one debriefing separately with its own leader. This might be useful for games played with cross-generation groups.

Don't labour it

There is a risk of players thoroughly enjoying the game, but learning to dread the debrief. So don't let it overrun; resist the temptation to plough through every one of the wonderful discussion points you have dreamed up. Remember that you want people to learn, and they learn more when they're interested and enjoying themselves than when they're shaking their watches.

For the same reason, always hold the debrief immediately after the game. Don't leave it to next week! No debrief is going to be exciting if it is merely chewing the stale bread of yesterday's fun.

What to do next

After the basic questions "what happened?" and "what can we learn?", there is a third: in the longer term — what do we do next?

You must ensure that you make the most of the interest aroused by the game. Games take a lot of your energy in preparation, thought, etc. It would be a shame if you didn't get all the returns possible on that investment.

So:

■ Ask the group if they want to look closer at any issue in the game.

■ Continue with some Bible studies on the passages considered during the game.

■ Reflect carefully afterwards on what happened in the game. What did it reveal about the interests and/or blind spots of your group? Is there anything there that you want to make the subject of future sessions?

What to do if a debriefing seems difficult

If a discussion in a debrief is going badly, or seems slow, this could be for a number of reasons:

■ The game may have flopped. If so, admit things have gone badly, and get the players' opinions on it all the same. Many groups will try to please you by not criticizing your precious game, so save time by being honest. It will lighten the air considerably. If you fear in advance this game may flop, you can always announce that the game is going to be a test. They are guinea pigs!

■ You may be trying to impose answers on the group. Go back to the beginning of this section. Do not pass "Go". Do not collect £200! If people do not feel their observations or contributions are being listened to and valued, they will quickly dry up. The object of the debrief is for them to talk, not you!

■ Check your questions to see they are open-ended. If the possible answers are "yes" or "no", they need some attention! The best questions are those that begin: "What. . .", "How . . .", "Why . . .", etc.

■ People's feelings may be too deep to express immediately. We don't expect that to apply to many of the games in this book. If it happens you can use one of the special debrief ideas described below. These can help a group that is finding it difficult to express feelings.

■ There may be an authority figure in the group who tends to dampen people's readiness to contribute. This has happened to us so often in youth groups that we are beginning to think it is a rule of sorts. The moment the minister, or one particular leader comes in to the discussion, the young people dry up. There are things you can do about it.

One is to exclude such figures from playing the game in the first place. And certainly no one should ever be there for the debrief who has not been fully involved in the game. No way can you accept "I'll just pop in for the last five minutes!"

A second is to split up for the debrief in such a way that the "villain" is in a smaller group, all of whom you know can cope with him/her.

■ The group may be *naturally* shy and diffident. (See also the box "Too much talking?") Again, you could try out some of the special debrief ideas, but discussion following them will still be difficult. Maybe you just have to agree your group are not a "games" group at the moment, and pick this book up again in a year's time.

Special debrief questions

Multiple choice

Questions such as "How do you feel?" can be so open-ended as to scare people. Why not rephrase it as a multiple choice question?
For example:

"During this game I felt

■ confused

■ angry

■ sad

■ happy

■ other . . ."

Unfinished sentence

Suggest a sentence they might finish: "The thing that most annoyed me (or that I most enjoyed) in this game was ⎯⎯⎯⎯⎯⎯⎯⎯⎯⎯⎯⎯⎯⎯⎯⎯

⎯⎯⎯⎯⎯⎯⎯⎯⎯⎯⎯⎯⎯⎯⎯⎯⎯⎯⎯⎯⎯⎯⎯⎯⎯⎯⎯⎯⎯⎯⎯⎯⎯⎯⎯⎯⎯ "

Pictures

Get people to choose a colour, draw a picture, or think of an animal, that somehow expresses what they feel.

Official secrets

Get everyone to write down an answer to a debrief question on a piece of paper and put it in an envelope and seal it. Then each group member attempts to wheedle out of another person what answers they put in that envelope. A time limit must apply after which the person has the option of revealing all. Or not. They usually will, and better discussion will follow.

So now you have mastered the art of debriefing — on to the games themselves.

Too much talking?

It might seem ironic that activity and participation is then followed by a return to words and discussion in which the articulate will once again excel, and some others will fade away into oblivion. We agree this can be a problem, but three things should be said:

1. If you spend enough time talking about "What happened?" then the less articulate are allowed to make their contributions more equally.

2. If a game has been good then people will want to talk about it — even those who are usually unwilling to contribute to discussion.

3. Because the initial experience has been shared, even those who say little can still gain from hearing the experience of others.

SECTION A

THE BIBLE

Although the aim of all the games in this book is to help explore the Bible, in this section we have particularly gathered those that focus on:

- Why the Bible is like it is
- Whether some bits are more important than others
- What we can learn from even the most obscure books

1. Little Bible

This seems an unlikely game. It's so simple it's hard to believe it works. It does though. Try it.

Imagine someone has asked you for a cut-down version of the Bible. What would it contain?

Time required

Playing time is between twenty-five and forty-five minutes. Debrief will take a further twenty minutes at least.

Suitable for

Teenagers and older. It works best with between twenty and forty players. They must have at least a "folk" knowledge of the Bible; it wouldn't do for a multi-faith group. The game goes well both with experts and with those who know only a little about the Bible, or with groups that combine both types. It has been played many times with adults *and* with teenagers.

Aims

1. To make players think about which bits of the Bible are most important to them, and how the various bits of the Bible balance out and fit together.

2. To allow players to realize for themselves that they don't actually know much about, say, the book of Amos, or about the differences between, say, Matthew and Luke, or 1 and 2 Corinthians. We think (but can't prove it of course) that players end up realizing how every book in the Bible has its place.

Preparation

Beforehand

1. The players will be split into teams of three people. Estimate how many teams you will have. Divide the number of teams by four. This gives you the approximate number of "Bible-packs" you will need to produce. If you are not sure how many teams you will have, or it doesn't divide exactly by four,

it is better to have too many "Bible-packs" than too few. (You can always have a couple of spares tucked away.)

A Bible-pack is a list of all the books in the Bible, the name of each book written clearly (felt-tip) on a separate slip of paper or record card. However, each Bible-pack contains three copies of Genesis, three copies of Psalms, and three copies of Mark, for reasons we explain later.

These Bible-packs are boring to produce, but don't take very long. No doubt you could use a photocopier or a word-processor to reduce the boredom, though probably not the time.

2. Mix all the Bible-packs together and shuffle well. Now shuffle again. Put them into a large envelope.

On the night

All you need is the shuffled Bible-packs, described above.

Playing the game

Split the players into teams of three. Left-over players are best put into teams of two people rather than four people.

Deal out the shuffled cards. Each team will get more or less the same number of cards — it's not important to get exactly the same number. They can look at their cards when they get them.

Briefing

Read out the following instructions:

The aim of the game is to make the best mini-Bible. You do this by swapping cards with other teams. You can make any bargains you like with other teams — swapping one for one, or one for many.

There are no winners or losers — it is up to you to do the best you can with your starting hand. Imagine that someone asked you for a cutdown version of the Bible; try and put together the most suitable collection of Bible books.

The easiest way to play is to lay your cards out in front of you, and for one player to stay with the cards. The other two players in the team can go out scouting for what is available for swapping from other teams.

One hint: don't be in too much of a rush to swap. Find out what is available first. Find out the going rate.

Then let the teams begin playing.

You will usually sense after a while that things are beginning to quieten down. When this happens, stop the game for a moment and ask each team, one at a time, to shout out what goods they still have on offer, or what they are still looking for. Then give a few more minutes open play.

At the end, allow some time for groups to wander around and look at other groups' results.

Variations

1. Not many variations. You can have some fun by adding non-existent Bible books (Hezekiah, Book of Rashes, Epistle to Dalmatians, Long songs of Moses) but·don't overdo this: the idea is not to make the players feel ignorant.

2. You can also give each team one joker card at the very end and let them use this as any book, to fill in a gap.

3. An additional dimension can be added to the game by the provision of independent Bible Information Controllers — BIC's for short — who are available to all groups to give very brief advice on the contents of unfamiliar books. This helps to overcome the problem that in some groups, particularly younger groups, this game could simply reinforce ignorance of the Bible instead of helping to overcome it.

These BIC's should know the Bible well *and* sympathize with the aims of the game. They should sit in a specified area of the room. Put a thirty-second limit on the information they can give to any enquirer. As far as possible they should aim to give exactly the same reply to exactly the same question so that they don't unduly influence the trading value of various books.

You can also put a limit on the number of "enquiries" each group can make. Give each group three BIC cards at the beginning of the game. They can trade each card for a piece of information from the BIC. But after they have used up their three cards they are on their own.

Debriefing (see page 20)

What happened?

1. What were the most popular books? The least popular?
Why?

2. Were there any absolutely essential books? Which ones? (You remember that there were extra copies of some books. They not only create more bargaining opportunities, but also give the players a chance to put a price on the "must have" books.)

What can we learn?

1. Does Matthew equal Mark equal Luke? If not, what are the differences?

2. What books did people feel they knew least about? Why is that?

3. What were the various teams trying to do when they chose books? Concentrate on balance? Or on the New Testament? Or the Gospels? Or the words of Jesus? Or Paul's letters?

4. Are some parts of the Bible more valuable than others? Leviticus? Minor Prophets? Revelation? Jude?
(N.B. Look at the box on Bible translation — "Which book first?")

5. Does your church make enough use of all parts of the Bible?

6. If you had to make a mini-Bible (of, say, fifteen books) what would be in it? Would it be the same for every possible reader?

Which book first?

When Bible translators begin, for the first time, to translate the Bible into a language that has no books of the Bible as yet, they are faced with just the same problems as we were in this game. Where do we start? What's most important?

Of course, the major translators such as Wycliffe Bible Translators and the United Bible Societies have a pattern. Usually the first book to be translated is Mark's Gospel, being the shortest, simplest, and most direct. Then follow, usually, another gospel or two, Acts, and a Pauline epistle — in that order. Next an Old Testament book — usually Genesis — is translated, followed by Psalms and then a prophet — probably Isaiah.

But there are some intriguing exceptions to this pattern. In 1948 an independent missionary, Frances Wakefield, translating the Bible into Tamahaq — the language of the Tuaregs, a nomadic people of the Sahara — started with Ruth, because it related so well to the way of life and the concerns of their society. She followed this up with Obadiah and Daniel for similar reasons, before ever getting to a gospel.

Similarly in 1957 James Torjeson, translating into Amis for a small group of people living in what is now Taiwan, began with James. It is always the needs of the local church and the situation they find themselves in, that must determine what is most relevant. Take a look at James and you will quickly be able to guess what some of the concerns of the Amis church must have been.

2. Connections

Youth workers are programmed to cope well with chaos. Young people are programmed to create it!

This game reverses those roles. The end result will be a riot of colourful cotton spreading around the room from wall to wall, to ceiling and floor. And in the process you will explore one of the most basic questions — "What connections are there between the Old Testament and the New Testament?"

Time required

Up to sixty minutes.

Suitable for

Groups which are able to find their way around the Bible, look up references, etc. Particularly suited to younger teenagers.

Aim

To help participants see the links between the Old and New Testaments.

Preparation

Beforehand

1. Obtain twelve reels of cotton — in three different colours — preferably yellow, red, and blue, or if you're feeling rich, wool is even better.

2. Supply Sellotape, Blu-tack, paper, felt-tipped pens, sticky labels, and a few Bibles for those who forget to bring one.

3. Warn everyone to bring a Bible to this activity.

4. Find a suitable room. Essential characteristics are:

■ Empty of furniture except for a few chairs

■ Larger than a badminton court

■ Four walls on which you can stick Sellotape

■ Solid rather than partition walls

5. Photocopy (or write out) one copy of each of the four lists of references below.

Group A		Group B		Group C		Group D	
MATTHEW	19.16–22	LUKE	4.16–21	1 CORINTHIANS	3.19	LUKE	4.4
ROMANS	3.10–12	ACTS	23.5	LUKE	4.25–27	MATTHEW	2.6
MARK	2.23–28	LUKE	9.18–20	ACTS	13.20	LUKE	9.54
HEBREWS	11.7	1 TIMOTHY	2.13	JOHN	13.1	MATTHEW	6.28–30
LUKE	23.45	MATTHEW	24.15	MATTHEW	24.29	LUKE	5.14
GENESIS	2.7	EXODUS	20.13–16	PSALM	14.1–3	1 SAMUEL	21.1–6
2 KINGS	5.1–14	GENESIS	6.13–22	EXODUS	26.31–33	ISAIAH	61.1–2
EZEKIEL	32.7	EXODUS	12.21–28	EXODUS	22.28	2 KINGS	2.1–18
MICAH	5.2	DEUTERONOMY	8.3	DANIEL	9.27	JOB	5.13
LEVITICUS	14.1–32	2 KINGS	1.9–16	1 KINGS	10.4–7	1 SAMUEL	3.20
LUKE	24.50–53	ACTS	17.16	JOHN	7.37–38	MARK	14.66–72
JOSHUA	1.9	GENESIS	1.1–2	EXODUS	3.4–6	RUTH	4.18–22

On the night

1. Clear away furniture if necessary.

2. Give each of the four "corners" a plastic bag containing one list of references, one reel of each colour of cotton, Sellotape, twelve sheets of paper, pens, and some Bibles.

Playing the game

Ask a few quick questions to get your group thinking about the Old Testament. Start with easy ones such as, "Name a book in the Old Testament".

Graduate to more difficult ones such as, "How many Old Testament books can you think of that are named after a person?"

Finally, throw out a challenge: "How many Old Testament books are quoted in the Gospels?" One answer is 14.

Then link, something like this:

"So the Old Testament and the New Testament are connected in lots of different ways. In this game we are going to explore those connections."

Briefing

Split into four different groups. It doesn't matter how, as the groups don't have to have equal numbers. How about, "What season were you born in? Winter go over to the corner near the piano. Spring by the window, etc. . . . ."

Each group goes to their "corner". They now "own" one wall of the room. The following three phases should be announced as described here, but you will also have to circulate, reminding each group in turn of what they must do next. They will work at very different speeds.

Phase 1 (10 minutes)

Look in your plastic bag. There you will find a list of twelve Bible references. Six of them are from the Old Testament and six are from the New Testament. The first thing to do is write out each reference (N.B. just the reference, not the whole passage) onto a separate sheet of paper and stick each sheet of paper to the wall behind you. Spread them all over the wall, not close together.

When this is almost done, get everyone's attention and announce the next two phases together.

Phase 2 (10 minutes)

Look up your New Testament references in a Bible. Each one connects in some way with one of the Old Testament references on another wall. You have to find out what connects with what. There might be lots of connections but to start with you only need to find one connection for each reference.

How are you going to find your connections? You could:

■ Look up all the Old Testament verses referred to and see if they connect to your New Testament ones

■ Use the notes in the margin of the Bible, if you have them

■ Use your own Bible knowledge and make inspired guesses

Phase 3

As soon as you have discovered a connection you then have to show it by stringing a piece of coloured cotton between your reference and the one to which it connects. Hold it . . . there are complications. You have three different coloured cottons. You have to use the right colour.
(N.B. Display these three statements on an overhead projector for reference.)

Blue if it is a quotation from the Old Testament
Red if it is a mention of a character from the Old Testament
Yellow if it is an idea/story/custom from the Old Testament
(Yellow is the most difficult.)

Stress that this is not a competition. They should not obstruct or interfere with the other groups. It is the total number of connections that matters. They can help the other teams to work out connections, if necessary. Leaders should circulate, discussing and commenting on connections, helping solve problems, and encouraging. By the end of these three stages — about twenty-five to thirty minutes, the room should be a glorious web of connecting cottons.

Phase 4 (optional)

What you do now depends very much on the interest and ability of your group. If the game has served your purpose then go straight to the debrief. If you wish to explore further then go on to either 1 or 2, below.

1. Using sticky labels, each group labels their connections (as illustrated) and indicates the theme or subject of the connection. This is demanding.

2. Have ten minutes of intense lateral thinking and try to establish as many connections as possible — obscure ones, obvious ones, funny ones, e.g. "These two connect because both begin with P", or "The two connect because the preacher last Sunday referred to both."

Debriefing (see page 20)

You might need to move into an uncluttered area of the room for this. This game has focused more on facts than on feelings or attitudes, so the debrief will not be such a crucial or lengthy component as in other games.

■ What happened?
■ What can we learn?

1. Did you face any problems using the Bible, e.g. finding references? Anything you can do about it?

2. Why are there so many connections?

3. Are you surprised?

4. The Old Testament was Jesus' Bible, and for centuries was the main written Scripture for Christians, as it still is for Jews. If they took (and take) it so seriously we can't afford to ignore it. What kind of things do we learn from the Old Testament? Get people to describe personal discoveries, not necessarily related to this game.

Other uses

You can use this model wherever the aim is to connect one item with another. It is at its best, however, where the connections are factual, rather than interpretative. So, for instance, our attempt to use this model for connecting the Bible with everyday situations today, met an untimely end.

There are subjects, however, where it can be useful. Connections between the four gospels — particularly their accounts of Holy Week; connections within the Old Testament — particularly between characters in different books, or between prophets and events in Old Testament history, can be a real help in visualizing the complex events of the Old Testament.

One dimension

In physical terms this may well be three-dimensional, but in content it is one-dimensional. It is a one-point game. Once the participants have got the point, and seen the wealth of connections between the Old Testament and the New Testament there is little point in prolonging the activity unless, of course, those connections can be further explored for their own sake.

We should not be afraid of such simple activities. And we should not try to overload them with meaning. That is why we have made phase 4 optional. It may well be that the extra detail would cause your group to lose the impact of what has gone before.

3. DIY Bible

Take a youth group — say twenty-five members. If each of them has been attending church for ten years, one service per week, then the group has together got about 12,500 hours of church experience! And that doesn't count all the extra meetings they've been to, such as Bible studies, socials, etc.

In this simulation the group distil that experience into a number of letters, drawings, stories, poems, and rules, each of which form their "manual of the church".

We call this "DIY Bible" because the process of forming the "manual of the church" has some fascinating similarities to the way the Bible was formed — so in a single weekend the group simulate some aspects of the process that took many hundreds of years to form the Bible we now use.

It's an exciting and creative way to deal with an enormous and difficult subject.

Time required

The six sessions fit a typical residential weekend:

Friday evening	Session 1	The problem page	1 hour
Saturday morning	Session 2	The rules	1 hour
	Session 3	My story	¼ hour
	Coffee		
	Session 4	Kulture	2 hours
Saturday afternoon	Session 5	The manual of the church	2 hours
Sunday morning	Session 6	The cover	1 hour
	Worship service		1 hour
Sunday afternoon	Debriefing		1 hour

Any one session can be used on its own (see Other uses, page 47).

Suitable for

Use at a residential weekend. All ages, all abilities, but participants must have had at least some experience of church life. When used with adults some activities will need adapting.

Preparation

Beforehand

1. You will need:

   ■ Plenty of paper, pens, felt-tipped pens, paints, pencils, rubbers, etc. for most sessions

   ■ Three (or more) different coloured A4 ring binders — one per eight participants

   ■ Scissors, hole-puncher, stapler, Blu-tack or equivalent

2. Read through the outline. Plan your weekend timetable around this structure, plan your introductions.

3. Prepare extra letters to Pat (as on page 39) for Session 1.

4. Prepare an overhead projector acetate or chart (as on page 43) for Session 4.

5. Recruit your assistant(s).

Playing the game

The leader's role throughout the weekend is to keep things running smoothly and to relate each session to the overall theme. So it is essential that you are familiar with the whole programme.

The simulation works at two levels: the obvious one — understanding and talking about the church; and the less obvious one — exploring how the Bible came into being. You must be aware of both levels as you go along, although, in our experience, it is part of the fascination that the links to the Bible gradually "click". We indicate in each session what the links are. Present this in your own way. We also include a suggested briefing for each session. Choose your own warm-ups as needed.

Session 1 — The problem page (1 hour, plus warm-ups)

The letters in the New Testament must be only a very small proportion of the letters that changed hands within the early church. Who knows? Maybe Paul ran a first century "problem page". It would be fascinating to see the original letters that provoked his replies. Just as the Bible contains letters, so "The manual of the church" will also contain letters.

1. Start with a suitable ice-breaking game (page 17).

2. Introduce the weekend — your aim at this point is to establish the importance of the task. It is not just a game. Participants must feel that what they are doing is much more than a "filler". In fact, it could change their lives and the lives of others.

The only predictable thing about this weekend is that it will be chaos — because what happens is up to you! We haven't got a speaker to bore you. Looking around I see that there are 30* people here. I would guess that each of you on average has attended some sort of church activity for two hours* a week for ten years*. So doing a quick calculation that means that between you, you have 30,000* hours of church experience. In all that time you must have learned a whole lot of things about the church. The aim of the weekend is to try to distil those 30,000* hours of church experience into some wisdom that will be worth passing on to others. We are going to create a manual of the church. And at the same time we are going to discover something about why the Bible is like it is.
(*Insert your own figures).

3. Introduce the task for this session

Pat (either a man or a woman) runs a problem page.

S/he is a very wise and spiritually mature person, always ready to listen, and very helpful. The task is to write a *short* letter to Pat about any real problem you face in your church. You won't have to read it out, and it will be as anonymous as your handwriting can be.

There is only one special rule — the letter must have a "but" in it. (N.B. This ensures the letter has both positives and negatives.) You have about twenty minutes.

Each person should do their own. During that time you should be on hand to help them understand the task, to assure them of its anonymity, and to announce how much time is left, at regular intervals. When they've finished, put the letters in a pile at the front of the room.

4. Now you are going to reply on behalf of Pat!

Everyone should grab one letter. Don't let them rummage through till they find an easy one — but do allow them to change if they think theirs is too difficult.

When finished, staple the reply to the original letter. Encourage people to browse through the letters and the replies.

Debriefing (see page 20)

When everyone has finished and has seen the reply to their own letter, discuss them. *This weekend must be debriefed as you go along.* There is no point in waiting until Sunday afternoon to discuss what happened on Friday night.

1. Did you find it easy to share your problem?
2. Was the answer helpful?
3. Why?/Why not?
4. How did you reply?
5. Could you see an answer to the problem even if it was like your own?

Session 2 – The rules (1 hour)

Preparation

Beforehand

Just as the Bible contains rules, so will "The manual of the church" contain rules which are specially relevant to us. So first of all tonight, as you sit down in front of the T.V., you will need to read all the letters to find out what problems they are describing. Make a list. For example, on a recent try-out we found the main "problems" were (no surprises here): 1. poor leadership; 2. the "generation gap"; 3. how to change things; 4. boring worship; 5. cliquey church; 6. irrelevance of the church to the "outside" world; 7. young people dropping out of church life; 8. lack of spiritual growth.

If all participants are from the same church you may find that many of the original letters discuss a similar issue. The task for the session is to create rules for people facing those problems, so you must now invent at least ten situations. Make them specific people in specific situations. For example, rules for:

A *young person* who wants to have influence on church decisions; or a *Minister* designing services for mixed-age congregations.

Write each situation on a separate piece of paper, and make two copies of each.

At the session

1. Begin with a warm-up.

2. Introduce the session

The first five books of the Bible contain many laws, regulations, and rules, as well as the early history of God's people. Rules have always been a necessary part of God's dealings with his people. Let's see what rules might be helpful for our manual of the church.

I worked hard last night. I read through all your letters, and discovered some of the problems which are bugging you. This morning we are going to think ourselves into those problems and draw up some rules for people in those situations.

Split into groups of three or four. If people come from different churches then each small group should contain a representative of at least two churches. If everyone is from the same church, then fix things a bit so that

cliques are broken down (the box below gives some ideas on how to do this).
Give each group one situation.

Splitting into groups

Random groups may be a good idea in theory, but in practice the groups tend to split in rather an unrandom, indeed predictable way. The gigglers get together. The artists get together. The intellectuals get together. The girls/boys get together, etc.

There are various ways to ensure more random or more balanced groups.

■ Split according to some outside random factor. E.g., if you want four groups, split according to the season in which people were born. Or, if the groups must be exactly equal in size, hand out playing cards (sorted so that they go spade, diamond, heart, club, spade, etc.) and group according to which suit you have been given.

■ Split according to some personal characteristics — e.g. hair colour, hair length, height, shoe-size, favourite colour, film, or fruit, etc. (out of a choice of four or five, or however many groups you want).

■ Staged split. Stage one is a natural split — then when these groups are formed, direct the next stage by instructing, for instance, that two from each group go to group one, two from each group to group two, etc.

■ If you want a distribution of skills then ask everyone who thinks they are good at drawing/good with words/good at glueing/good at helping others/good at asking questions/good at nothing, to get into groups, then get one or two people from each group into new groupings.

■ Sometimes there is no alternative but to allocate so that one key person is in each group.

■ Point out what kind of split you want and just trust your participants to split appropriately.

3. Once the groups are assembled, give a few guidelines:

■ Each rule must start with the word "you"

■ Draw up at least three rules for that situation, but more if you like

■ Agree about each rule (but if a group gets bogged down suggest each member proposes one rule)

When they finish one set of rules, give them another situation as different as possible from their first. In forty-five minutes fast groups will write about three sets of rules, slow groups, one. Allow fifteen minutes to debrief.

Debriefing

Collect the rules, then get into two separate groups for a quick discussion:

1. Was it difficult?
2. Did you make positive or negative rules?
3. Did you have to assume who was to blame in your situation?
4. How can you set rules for yourselves?

Session 3 – My story

1. Introduce the task (15 minutes)

   The bits of the Bible that we know best are the stories. Many of these stories were simple Hebrew family stories shared around a campfire. Our manual of the church is to include some of the simple stories of our everyday Christian experiences. The sort of things we might share over a cup of coffee. So write a quick story, as short as you want, of any time that God, Jesus, or the Church has meant something good to you. It must be true and it must be honest. Don't put your name on it, so it will be as anonymous as your writing.

   Give them as long as they want to finish. They are unlikely to need more than ten minutes. Then have a coffee break.

2. (Optional.) Ask them to write at the bottom of their story, a Bible text, story, character, or incident which they feel helps to explain their story.

Debriefing

Because people finish at different times it has never been practical to talk about this session together. Reserve any observations you have made and briefly discuss this activity at the beginning of the next session.

Session 4 – Kulture (2 hours)

Remind the group of the purpose of this weekend — to distil our 30,000 hours' church experience into "The manual of the church". The Bible contains poems, proverbs, parables, songs, and drama. Mine even contains pictures. So, too, will "The manual of the church".

1. Introduce the session

   Between now and lunchtime, create something artistic — a poem, a picture, a song, a sketch — anything to help the reader/observer to think about what the church really is. Do as many as you want, on your own, or in a group.

   It is our experience that by this stage they will no longer be thinking in the narrow "church" terms but about the whole scope of Christian experience. This can be an immensely valuable session.

2. Display on an overhead projector a list of some Kulture ideas — e.g. cartoon, joke, chorus, song, graphics, of the words "Our church", a logo, a drama sketch (to be written down as fully as possible — they might need somebody to watch and help them write it down), symbol, drawing, collage, strip-cartoon story, dream, poem.

It can help to give people poem structures:

E.g. 1. *Haiku*, which is a simple seventeen-syllable description in three lines of five, seven, and five syllables. For example:

> Churches? – people think
> of choirs and spires. Me, I think
> of open doorways

E.g. 2. Limerick

E.g. 3. Another five-line poem that has:

	for example:
a noun (preferably a short one)	church
an -ing word	hoping
a five-syllable line describing the noun	listens...silently
another -ing word	waiting
the same noun	church

Encourage each person to produce two items — in two different styles if possible.

As the items are finished collect them, or stick them up on the wall. Now it's time for some well-earned lunch!

Session 5 – The manual of the church (2 hours)

Time off? No chance. Send everyone else packing while you prepare for session 5, in which three or more groups select, from the many items so far created, eight that they want for their manual.

Preparation

Count how many items have been created so far. Don't throw any out — leave that to the participants. From a group of twenty-five you might expect:

25 letters and replies
17 sets of rules
25 stories
<u>23 kulture</u>
90 total

You will need one selection group for every thirty items.

Saturday afternoon on a residential weekend is often difficult. People are tired. They have been out in the fresh air. They are hungry. Usually the speaker has run out of steam.

Not so on a DIY Bible weekend. Now it starts to get especially interesting, as "The manual of the church" begins to appear out of the mass of material so far created.

Warming up

You will need to start with a game or two to establish concentration. Try a move maker from page 18. Follow this with "Arguments" — (page 19).

1. Still in pairs, introduce the next task.

From the vast amount of literature available to the early church we can imagine that God spoke to the church through some of it more than the rest. Our Bible, we might say, contains the pieces God particularly wanted to speak through.

In the same way our manual of the church is going to contain a small part of all the material we have available. We are going to discuss together which of the pieces leads the church in God's direction.

Over the weekend so far you have produced (nearly one hundred) items which represent some of your opinions, feelings, attitudes, advice, and wisdom on the subject of the church.

Which of these do you want to include in your manual? The question is not "Is it good?" but "Does it lead us in some way in God's direction?"

N.B. You could, if you wish, relate the task more to the services which will follow on Sunday morning — i.e. "Select items which you think should be used at the service on Sunday morning". This makes the task more concrete.

2. Put the items into four piles — *letters, rules, stories, kulture*. Each pair gets the same number of items, including at least one from each pile. They should discard the two least useful items, and put the rest in an agreed order of usefulness.

3. Pairs get together as groups of eight (or more), around a table. On each table place a different coloured ring binder.

Elect a chairperson and then agree unanimously which eight items (or ten if optional stage 4 is used) are to be included in your manual. The criterion is — "Does it help lead the church in God's direction?" Note also:

■ Every manual must include at least one *letter*, one *rule*, one *story* and one item of *kulture*

■ Think about the merit of each item, but also the balance of the manual as a whole

On one occasion we used "blockers" (see page 127), one planted in each group. This helped to sharpen the group's perception of the task.

From the discards from stage 2, choose any that you think deserve to be given further consideration and feed them back into groups — a maximum of two per group.

4. (Optional.) When the final selection of ten has been made, the manuals are passed to another group who must remove one item which in their opinion is least helpful. Pass the manual to another group, who remove one further item. Return the manuals to the original owners, who note what has been removed.

It may be that there were not enough "good" things to make up a whole manual, in which case this phase can significantly improve the whole selection. But the real purpose of this optional phase is to introduce the idea of disagreement as to what should be in the Bible. For example, both Protestants and Catholics can be hurt by the inclusion or exclusion of the Deuterocanonical Books/Apocrypha. This fact is obviously implied in the whole simulation, but is made all the more poignant by the fact that after a group had reached consensus on what should be included, other groups then changed things.

5. Each group thinks of a title for each item, and puts the items in the best order; tidies them up by cutting off rough edges; thinks of a title for the whole selection, and prepares a title page for the manual.
(N.B. not a cover, which is left to session 6.)

Debriefing

This session should take about two hours. It will be quite exhausting for all concerned and a debrief may be difficult in the circumstances — but at least try to gather feedback to the following questions — either in small groups of six (across the choosing groups) or in plenary.

■ What happened?

1. How did you feel about that activity?
2. Was it easy or difficult to agree?
3. How did you feel about your own items being chosen or discarded?

Session 6 – The cover (1 hour)

If the manuals are to be used in a service you may want to split the groups at this stage — one group to prepare the service, the other to make covers for the manuals.

The covers

The group working on the covers should make the manuals as attractive as possible. Also encourage them to think of the questions:

- Who is the manual for?
- What are their interests?
- How can the cover best relate to their interests?

The service

If items are to be read or used at the service, you may find the following points helpful:

- Have the manuals on a table at the front of the church — when people come to read from them they take the manual from there and return it to there
- Use about ten-to-fifteen minutes-worth of the manual material, preceded by a simple explanation of the way the game worked and the purpose behind it
- Get the preacher to preach about the way the Bible was formed, and the value of it to the Christian

---

The preacher

When we have used this simulation we have had control of the service — and it has proved to be an indispensable part of the process of debriefing. The presentation of the manual, the recap of the game and an explanation of its objectives seem to trigger the group into debriefing the game for themselves. People say "Everything dropped into place", "It all made sense this morning", etc. What happens if you do not have that control we do not know, so do all you can to get it. In our experience it has also been useful to have outsiders at the service who know nothing of the weekend other than what is presented at the service. It gives clarity to the presentation.

Debriefing (see page 20)

This activity must be debriefed as you go along. However, we have always reserved the final session after lunch on Sunday for a discussion of what has happened, and how it relates to the Bible and to them.

You might find it helpful to start off with small groups of six.

- What happened?
- What can we learn?

The church

1. What do you want to change in your church?
2. How can it be changed?
3. What role do you have to play in your church?

The Bible

1. How is your manual like/unlike the Bible?

This game is in no way a strict parallel of the process of forming the Bible — and, of course, it does not pretend to be. It raises issues, however, and this debrief can investigate various similarities and differences between the manuals and the Bible:

■ The Bible contains letters, rules, stories, and songs, just as our manuals do

■ In the time of the early church there were many letters, gospels, and writings which might or might not have become part of the New Testament

The church leaders did not conduct a selection panel like ours, but we can imagine them constantly asking the questions "What is God saying to the church through this writing?", "Does this help us grow in faith and remain true to Christ?", "Does it, in fact, lead us in God's direction?"

One key component of all New Testament writings is the link with the apostles. But there is still a process of choosing. And the test applied is much less, "Is this good literature?", much more "Is this what God wants to say to us?", and "Has this already proved its usefulness in the church?"

■ The writers of the New Testament talked about being inspired by the Holy Spirit. Unfortunately our game could not simulate that part of the process. We always find, however, that one of the most lively aspects of the debrief is the role of the Holy Spirit. How did the Holy Spirit inspire the Bible writers? How did he inspire the church leaders?

■ Covers and titles highlight the question, who is our manual for? The same question can be asked, who is the Bible for — just for Christians? Or can everyone learn from it?

■ If you added the optional extra in session 3, the point is that many of the New Testament writers introduced the Old Testament in this way. They referred people to, or quoted, Old Testament texts and stories that supported or connected with their subject.

So the New Testament is packed full of references to the Old. For example, Acts 2.16–21; Luke 3.4–6; Romans 3.10–18.

Other uses

1. The subject that we have used throughout — "The church" — is only one possibility. A manual could be prepared on worship, families,

relationships, Jesus, or peace, for example. The main requirement is that the subject should be one familiar to the participants, and one which can be approached from all the different angles that this simulation requires.

2. If you choose another subject you may choose to ignore the reflections on how the Bible came to be formed. These might, in any case, be less relevant for your group than the opportunity this game gives for you to explore one particular area of Christian life.

3. Any of the sessions can be used on its own. If you wish to use session 5 on its own, you will have to provide something to choose from! You can use any of the following: photocopies of Bible passages; postcards of famous religious pictures/stained glass; religious posters; hymns; poems — from Steve Turner to T.S. Eliot via John Betjeman; meditations; famous passages from books; prayers; sermons; letters from magazines; some real Christian problem page such as in *Jam*; or you could create all the ninety odd items yourself if you've got a masochistic streak!

Best seller (opposite) treats the subject matter of session 6 in more detail.

4. Best seller

When visiting a youth group in Liverpool, Jim had taken with him the latest Bible published by the Bible Society. One young man picked it up eagerly, but after one look inside, put it down with obvious disappointment. "What's wrong with it?"

"It's got two columns," he replied, "No paperback has two columns. Why can't you produce a Bible like an ordinary book? And what about the cover? What I'd really like is a Bible which looked modern like a novel, so I could read it on the train without everyone thinking I was some sort of religious nut!" Good point! We could spot a Bible from one hundred yards in the light of a single street lamp.

In this game you create a new cover for the Bible. In the process you have to decide, what is the message of the Bible? Who is the Bible aimed at? Is it suited to the best seller treatment? Should it have a multi-coloured cover with shiny silver lettering, or one of those soft focus sunsets? Most of all, what kind of cover would really make people want to "enquire within"?

Time required

Up to two hours.

Suitable for

Any group of "thinking" Christians, young or old — particularly those with an interest in outreach. Artistic ability helps, but is not essential.

Aims

1. To increase awareness of the "message" of the Bible.
2. To consider who that message is for.

Preparation

Beforehand

1. Get lots of artistic materials together — paints, gold and silver felt-tipped pens, paper, coloured card, silver paper, glue, Sellotape, ruler, Biros, Letraset, etc. — as much as you can afford.

2. Get together a selection of Bibles. Raid your bookshelves and your friends' bookshelves to get Bibles with all sorts of covers — black leather, zipped, sunsets, photographs, full colour, etc.

3. Book a room that can withstand the messiness of painting, etc.

4. Gather lots of magazines with photos in them.

5. Choose audiences from the list below, and prepare a label for each.

Youth groups	*Adult groups*
Members of my class at school	Customers at a station bookstall
Friends at work/college	Business people in hotel
Heavy metal freaks	bedrooms
People who listen to Radio 1	Readers of romantic fiction
People who live in bed-sits	Readers of *Financial Times*
Unemployed people	Alcoholics
Lonely people	People on a diet
Drug addicts	Peace campaigners
Members of other religions	Members of the armed forces
People on package holidays in	People who do crosswords
Spain	Parents with young children
	Very rich people
	Poor people

6. Prepare one copy of the briefing instructions for each player (see opposite page).

7. Visit a jumble sale and buy a few Bible-sized books.

On the night

1. Set up your room with large work spaces — put two or three tables together if necessary.

Playing the game

Unusually, we begin this activity with a discussion. We have found that the most important obstacle to overcome is the prejudice that this is going to be a Sunday school colouring activity!

Hold up a Bible that looks like a Bible — black leather — and ask what it is. Of course everyone knows — why?

Thus introduce the question of whether a Bible has to look like that. Could it not look like this . . ? or this . . ? and show some other Bibles. In fact, what is it that determines what a Bible cover looks like? Encourage people to suggest reasons.

Briefing instructions (one copy for each person)

Oaktree publishing, creators of the New Universal translation of the Bible (the NU for short), have commissioned you to work on a design for the new NU range of Bibles.

They are producing NU editions for various target audiences (you will be told which audience you are to work on).

They want the NU Bible to look more like an ordinary book than a traditional Bible.

The cover should have three components:

1. A title.

2. A byline — less than ten words which explain why this book is valuable and worth reading.

3. Some illustration — for example a photo or drawing.

Points to note

1. You will have been provided with a book to which you can glue your cover, so make sure your cover is the right size.

2. Discuss together how you approach this task before launching into the design.

Try to establish that:

■ It must reflect what's inside

■ It must appeal to the people who are going to buy or read it

Warming up

Use any game that creates some sense of artistic endeavour. A version of charades that uses pictures instead of mime would be one possibility. Or alternatively try a drawing game, such as the following from *Picture It!*

Give each person a piece of paper and a pencil. Sit them in a circle. Each person must draw a picture of the person opposite them. But there's a catch — they cannot look at the paper, and they cannot lift the pencil from the paper. The results usually look quite extra-terrestrial.

Briefing

The design committee of a big Bible publisher — Oaktree Publishing — has asked you to help them in designing a Bible for a particular group of

readers. They want the cover of the Bible to attract the readers, and to express to the readers something of what the Bible is about.

Hand out the briefing instructions.

They don't want the Bible to look like a traditional Bible, but to look more like an ordinary book.

The cover should have three components:

1. A title.

2. A byline — less than ten words which explain why this book is valuable and worth reading.

3. Some illustration — for example a photo or a drawing.

Each of you has been asked to design a Bible for different readers. Once you are in groups I will hand you a card which shows who your readers are.

You will need to think hard about those readers — what do they like doing? What do they most need? What do they think of the Bible, or of Jesus? What is there in the Bible which might help them?

Phase 1 (up to 45 minutes)

Players get into groups. They can be in pairs or threes. Hand each group a card showing their intended readers. Some may want to change their card. Discourage this unless there seems a good reason to change.

Now let them get on with the task. Help them, if need be, to do the necessary thinking about titles, audiences, image.

Give regular time-checks. Around ten minutes before the end remind them that they should stick their cover onto the Bible-sized book.

Phase 2 (10 minutes)

Display the finished books around the room. Number them.

Gather all the audience cards — including those that were not used. Invite people to match up the audiences with the various covers. Stress that the point is not "how good?" but "for whom was this intended?"

Debriefing (see page 20)

What happened?

This has not been an interactive game, so many of the usual debrief questions might not apply. But discuss:

■ What made the task easy/difficult?

■ Were some audiences easier than others?

■ How did you decide things in your group?

What can we learn?

1. Take each cover in turn, and invite all those who were not involved in making it, to say what they think the cover's trying to convey, and what they think it actually conveys.

2. Why is the Bible such a best seller? Why do people not read it much?

3. Does what the Bible looks like actually matter?

4. Communicating Christian faith is best done by personal contact, rather than by a book or literature. What part might the Bible have to play in Christian communication?

A book?

We have often got youth workers to think of a subtitle for the Bible. Nearly always the idea of a book remains in the title — "Manual", "Guidebook", "Handbook", "Encyclopaedia". But although the Bible is a book, the words of God are not. This game will throw up such observations. The fact that a book becomes the centre of attention is obviously a barrier to those who are not into books. How can we release the words of God from the book?

---

5. Mix'n'match

We read somewhere that priests are trained to look up when they reach the key point of the Gospel passage they are reading out loud. In this way at least something is driven home to the listeners.

Perhaps your experience is, like ours, of a distressingly large number of monotonously read Bible passages, treated like a school exercise, with the reader out front hardly aware that he or she has a duty to make the words of the Bible live as though they were brand new.

This game is fun to play — a simple idea, which catches fire well — yet has a lot to say about listening, really listening, to the Bible.

Time required
About forty minutes.

Suitable for
Any age, from young teenagers up. The players should have some interest in the teaching of the Bible. The complexity of the passage chosen can help determine how suitable it is for adults.

Aims
1. To make the players very familiar with the teaching of a particular Bible passage.

2. To raise questions about how effectively they listened to the passage when it was read without any special warning.

Preparation

Beforehand

1. Choose the passage you want to use. It should be between, say, fifteen and twenty-five verses. Choose a passage which has a coherent theme, but not a narrative passage. Something from an epistle is ideal, or a psalm might work.

The passage should not be utterly straightforward, but neither excessively complex. It is better to be too complex than too simple. For example: Romans 8.1–30; 1 Corinthians 14.1–25; Philippians 3.1–21; Hebrews 5.11 — 6.12; James 2.14–26.

2. Type out the verses of the passage *in the wrong order*. (Don't number the verses!) Leave a couple of blank lines between each verse. If the verses are quite long, feel free to break them up into bits, and shuffle them around, too.

3. Type some of the verses again, but with the meaning altered subtly — for example add the word "not" or "sometimes", or change "will" into "may".

4. Type one or two verses on the same subject, but from other Bible passages.

5. Make one or two verses up, if you feel like it.

6. Now photocopy these. Players will be in teams of three. Each team will need one copy of the photocopy.

7. Cut up each copy along the blank lines between the verses. Put each cut-up copy in a separate envelope. So each envelope contains the entire passage and the extra verses, cut up.

(*Warning to clever-clogs*: don't try and save time by simply photocopying the original passage and then cutting it up, because the players will simply fit it back together along the scissor-lines. You have to type it out in the wrong order to start with. Yes it is boring, but if you're such a clever-clogs you should know how to touch type anyway.)

On the night

1. Provide one envelope per team, containing the cut-up passage.

2. Provide a small lump of Blu-tack per team, which they will use to stick down the pieces in what they hope is the correct order. They can stick them onto the wall if it is a friendly sort of wall, or onto another piece of paper.

Playing the game

Say nothing about the game. Read through the (unmuddled) passage, from the Bible. Check that there was nothing people found hard to understand. Ask if there are any questions about the passage. Perhaps make a few comments about it.

Then split the group into teams of three and hand out the envelopes with the following instructions:

In the envelope is the passage you just said you understood. It has been muddled up. Also some extra verses and some wrong verses have been added.

You must weed out the extra verses and the wrong ones, and then try and put the muddled verses into the correct order.

Give the teams a few minutes warning before they must finish, and get them to stick their versions down with the Blu-tack.

Close the game by getting some teams to read out their versions, and by finding out which verses have been weeded out. Then read through the correct version.

You will find that closing the game leads very naturally into the debrief — which should be kept short, as most of the learning has already taken place.

Variations

1. With more advanced groups you can leave one or two verses out, and get them to recreate them from memory.

2. To be really difficult, you can read the passage from a version of the Bible different from the one you photocopied, or use a paraphrase (e.g. *Living Bible*).

3. If your group meets after a church service, then you can use the passage read during the service, without reading it again. (This assumes you can find out well enough in advance what it is going to be.)

Debriefing (see page 20)

What happened?

1. Is it an easy game to play? What in particular makes it difficult?

2. What were the most difficult things to understand in the passage?

What can we learn?

1. Should Bible passages be read out loud? Were they originally meant to be?

2. How could a Bible passage be made easier to understand when it is being read out loud?

6. Give us a proverb

The proverbs defy description, mixing as they do humanist philosophy, common sense, spiritual insight, cynicism, and worldliness. But one thing they constantly repeat — if you listen to good advice you will learn to live a more godly life. This game sets out both to "listen" to some Bible proverbs, and to create our own. It helps to isolate some themes and to provide a fun introduction to one of the under-used books of the Bible. Preparation is slightly complex. But after that it runs like the popular party game of charades, with a few refinements, and (if you wish) an extra phase added on.

Time required

Up to half-an-hour, then another thirty minutes for the optional phase.

Suitable for

Any group of people, young or old, used to playing charades. Use it at a party, or to start off a Bible study or a discussion.

Aims

1. To identify some themes running through the various proverbs.

2. To learn "how to live intelligently and how to be honest, just, and fair". (Proverbs 1.3)

Preparation

Beforehand

1. Decide how many proverbs to use — which will be determined by the time available.

2. Select from the following list. Write, or better still type, the proverbs you have selected on to a single sheet of paper.
N.B. Ignore the brackets for the time being. The significance of the brackets is explained in point 3. Number each proverb. This is now your "master list". Get four copies of it.

Proverbs

1. Someone who (holds back) the (truth) causes (trouble), but one who openly (criticizes) works for (peace). 10.10

2. (Reverence) for the LORD gives (confidence and security) to a (man) and his (family). 14.26

3. When people are (happy), they (smile), but (when they are sad), they (look depressed). 15.13

4. The LORD wants (weights and measures) to be (honest) and every (sale) to be (fair). 16.11

5. Kings cannot (tolerate evil), because (justice) is what makes a (government) strong. 16.12

6. Better to eat a (dry crust of bread) with (peace of mind) than to have a (banquet) in a house (full of trouble). 17.1

7. . . . (Remembering wrongs) can (break up a friendship). 17.9

8. Some people (ruin themselves) by their own (stupid actions) and then (blame the LORD). 19.3

9. If you are (sensible), you will (control your temper). When someone (wrongs you), it is (a great virtue) to (ignore) it. 19.11

10. When you (give to the poor), it is like (lending to the LORD), and the LORD will (pay you back). 19.17

11. (Drinking) too much makes you (loud and foolish). It's (stupid to get drunk). 20.1

12. A (gossip) can never (keep a secret). Stay away from people who (talk too much). 20.19

13. The more easily you (get your wealth), the (less good) it will do you. 20.21

14. (Better) to live (on the roof) than (share the house) with a (nagging wife). 21.9

15. Singing to (a person who is depressed) is like (taking off his clothes) on a (cold day) or like (rubbing salt in a wound). 25.20

16. Some people are (too lazy) to put (food in their own mouths). 26.15

17. (Human desires) are like the (world) of the (dead) — there is always (room for more). 27.20

18. (Discipline) your son and you can always (be proud of him). He will never give you reason (to be ashamed). 29.17

19. There are four things that are too mysterious for me to understand: an (eagle) flying in the sky, a (snake) moving on a rock, a (ship) finding its way over the sea, and (a man and a woman falling in love). 30.18–19

20. (Charm) is deceptive and (beauty) disappears, but a woman who (honours the LORD) should be (praised). 31.30

3. It is a little more difficult to guess a twenty-word proverb than a film, or book titles. So we have made it a bit easier.

Each group will be given the list of proverbs but with all the important verbs, nouns, and a few other words, missed out. So take one copy of your list, and white out with ''Tippex'' the words the teams are going to have to guess. On our sample list we have indicated these words in brackets. At its most basic, with one word alone missed out, this game could be played with the most inexperienced group. The more words you white out, the more difficult the game becomes.

Then get one photocopy of this list per group.

4. Take a copy of your original master list — one per group — and cut each list into slips each carrying a single proverb. Mix each team's slips so they are in a random order. Get a clipboard and rig it up like this:

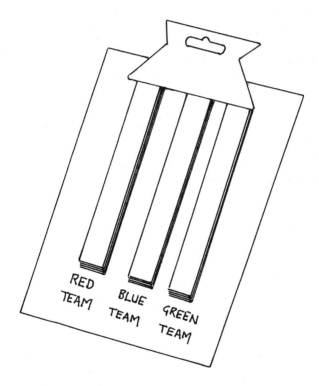

On the night

1. Write out your example proverbs as on page 58 (with gaps) on an overhead projector. Get a volunteer to help you introduce the game.

2. Display the following list of categories:
- Family relationships
- Business life and public life
- Personal relationships and friendship
- Attitude to others
- Relationship with God
- Personal qualities

Briefing

Read out, not in a "Here is the lesson" type-of-way, but in a "party-master-of-ceremonies" type-of-way, Proverbs 1.1–6. Then:

I have a list here of twenty selected proverbs from the book of Proverbs. You are going to split into three teams (or more), and try to find out what I have written here. Just like in charades, one of you comes to find out the proverb, and returns to your group to mime it. No Bibles are allowed. I have picked proverbs that are particularly good fun to mime, but which also represent the main themes we see in the book of Proverbs.

One person from the group come and get the first proverb. To make it easy each of you have a list of these proverbs, and all you have to do is to fill in the gaps, by miming the words or phrases that are missing. One person record your solutions. Once you have fully guessed your proverb, come back for another one.

Finally, when you have guessed all the proverbs, you have to decide as a group which, of the categories displayed up here, each proverb belongs to. It may belong to more than one.

Then show an example:

(Beauty) in a (woman) without good judgement is like (a gold ring) in (a pig's snout). 11.22

or

It is better to meet (a mother bear) robbed of (her cubs) than to meet (some fool) busy with (a stupid project). 17.12

Get a volunteer to mime, while all the participants guess.

All the useful charade rules apply — phrase length; number of words; number of syllables; sounds like; shorter; longer; — all have recognized signs. After that it is the quality of the mime that counts.

Originality is to be commended!

Playing the game

This is the easy part. Get into three teams, red, green, and blue. One person from each group gets a slip carrying a proverb. They need to take the slip with them — as otherwise they are bound to forget some words and come back to ask you — but they must not show the slip to anyone in the group.

They must start by indicating which number the proverb is on the list (1 — 20) with their fingers — or fingers and toes!

When one group has finished and has allocated each proverb to a category, bring everybody back together.

Variations

See "Give us a proverb" — the optional extra that follows below.

Debriefing

This need not be formal. The game is too light for that. Look at what happened, as usual. Then get each team to go through their categorization of the proverbs.

Then turn to particular proverbs:

1. Which ones surprised you? Amused you? Touched you? Angered you?

2. When the proverb writer said his proverbs help people to live intelligently, justly, and fairly, what did he mean? How would these help? Which ones would help most?

3. What are the most obvious differences between the world of the proverb writer, and our world? How should those differences affect how we read the book of Proverbs?

Other uses

It will be obvious to you that the same treatment could be used on any sayings in the Bible. But avoid using it with favourite "texts" as it would encourage seeing texts out of context.

Give us a proverb — an optional extra

Proverb writers learn about life from looking at the way life itself is, which distinguishes them from, say, the prophets, who look at life from God's standpoint and bring a message direct from God.

So unlike prophecy, which is a particular gift from God, creating proverbs is something that all of us are well qualified to try out. We can all observe life as it is, and draw our conclusions about what is good, right, true, and proper.

Thus this final optional phase which aims to create totally original proverbs based on our own experience — yet proverbs which reflect on some of the six areas of life studied in the game:

1. Family relationships
2. Business life and public life
3. Personal relationships and friendship

4. Attitude to others
5. Relationship with God
6. Personal qualities

We suggest this phase is optional because while the game itself was deliberately designed to work with all kinds of groups aged from twelve upwards, this phase will work only with those who have the capacity to distance themselves a little bit from what they see around them, and so to reflect upon what they see.

Running the activity

1. Split into twos or threes.

2. The aim is to create proverbs on some of the subject areas that proverbs in the Bible deal with. Each group has a choice from the list of six subject areas we used in the game. Choose two which you would like to create modern proverbs on.

(Find out what's been chosen. If one area has been neglected completely, maybe suggest one group picks that up as an extra.)

3. Now spend ten minutes sharing with the others in your group your observations on this area of life. One of you will need to take some notes. These questions may help focus your discussion:

What makes you really sad about . . . (subject area) . . . today?
What makes you really happy about . . . (subject area) . . . today?

Then, after ten minutes discussion:

4. Now let's see if you can turn those observations into proverbs. Your proverbs can take any form you want, but if you need some help here are some typical "structures" for proverbs in the Bible:

Display the following on an overhead projector:

■ First, there are proverbs that give the reader a choice between two options:

"It is better to . . . than to . . ."
"You may think that . . . , but really . . ."
". . . sort of people are . . . but . . . sort of people are . . ."

■ Others suggest how certain results follow from certain behaviour:

"Do that . . . and you will . . . But do this . . . and you will . . ."
"Do you want . . . then . . ."

■ Then there are others which simply make statements:

"The Lord hates . . ."
"The Lord is pleased with . . ."

You might also give some modern examples of your own. Here are two recent and highly poignant ones:

■ Family relationships:

Nothing is sadder than divorced parents squabbling over who keeps the children.

■ Business life and public life:

Better to make bread to feed the hungry than to make arms to kill the weak.

5. Allow another fifteen minutes for proverb-writing. Then get each group to share its proverbs, and write them up on a flip chart or overhead projector.

6. Close by inviting everyone to choose which of the final list they would most like to memorize and take away with them.

SECTION B

THE CHRISTIAN COMMUNITY

Our lives together as Christians in churches, youth groups, social groups, etc. is a rich source of material for simulations.

The games which follow in this section look at relationships, decision making, roles, and priorities within the body of Christ.

They particularly look at how we can bring the teaching of the Bible, sometimes so remote from us, right into the centre of our lives together as Christians.

7. Matching game

At first sight this might appear to be the odd-game-out. Every other game in this book includes a Bible study element *within the game itself*. This one does not. Instead, it suggests a game to play in one session, then a Bible exploration for you to try out in the week following the game. Why include such a game in this book?

Obviously the subject of this game — boy/girl relationships, and in particular the hectic pairing and parting of adolescence — is important and powerful enough to merit a place in any book for youth work.

We all know how deeply the quality of relationships can affect the life of a youth group. St Paul, indeed, found as much in the churches he wrote to. See how often his letters include little asides encouraging people to settle arguments, helping to soothe hurt feelings, or dealing with some issues of sexual morality. He knew, as well as we do, that insecure relationships can hinder the work of the kingdom.

Now insecure relationships are, almost by definition, a feature of adolescence. Which is all the more reason to ensure that your group is helped to identify, appreciate, and deal with some of these insecurities. The "Matching game" won't remove the insecurities, but it will help you shine some light of biblical teaching upon them.

However, there are two other important reasons why this game is in the book:

1. It's in the book because it's a useful game "model". (There is more about this in "Designing your own games" on page 138).

For the methodologically minded, therefore, the theory behind this game's use of the Bible is:

■ We analyse people's situation to see what are some of the distinctive stresses and strains of boy/girl relationships today

As we said earlier, Bible teaching does not occur in a vacuum, and nor should our exploration of the Bible occur in a vacuum. Often the first task of a game is to identify an area of need, or an issue, or a problem to which the biblical data can be applied.

■ We explore a range of biblical material — both practical examples, and "teaching" — on the subject of relationships

■ We attempt to draw up a biblical "action plan" — in this case a set of "commandments for relationships" — which the participants can take back with them into the situations they identified in the game, and which will — we hope — affect their subsequent approach to dating

2. It's in the book because it illustrates some problems we face when there is a particularly great distance between our society and the society originally addressed by the Bible.

The Bible is about relationships. God relates to us human beings. We relate to each other. So, logic would suggest, it would be an excellent place to look for advice and guidance on all aspects of human relationships.

Now up to a point that is obviously true. But when it comes to boy or girl friends, being a teenager now is rather different from the time of St Paul and Jesus. In those days most people were already married by the time they reached their late teens, and often it was to someone chosen by their families. Teenage relationships were not an issue, therefore to the eager ears of a teenager the Bible appears almost silent on the subject. Particularly when they compare it with the amount of time that TV, music, films, and friendly chat devote to it.

Advice is available from all quarters. The problem page offers endless tips on how to get the partner you want; how to keep him/her; how to behave sexually. And it's our guess that although many youth workers might often wish to disagree with the advice offered in the teenage magazines, we do, almost without exception, welcome their openness, directness, and honesty.

Such directness, however, sets up an expectation in the teenager that all guidance in the area of relationships will be offered with the same candour. Which poses us with a problem when it comes to the Bible. Put yourself, for a moment, in the shoes of one of your teenage youth-group members who comes to the Bible for advice on relationships. The problem page may lead them to expect it will take on the mantle of the confident agony aunt offering specific judgements. "It's OK to kiss." "Watch out for petting." "Masturbation is . . .", etc.

But the Bible, we all know, is not like that. Its advice on relationships, though very specific where it impinges on the life-styles of the time, is not always easy for young people to understand — for any of us to understand. It doesn't seem to anticipate the crisis of an adolescent faced by the big question — "How do I behave myself on my first date?" "What is normal?" "What is right?"

So when we set out to provide a game that looked at some aspects of relationships we decided that we should try to ensure that the game:

■ Recognized that specific Bible teaching on some matters that are of most interest to teenagers is sometimes non-existent, and often elliptical

■ Yet which recognized that the best recipe for good relationships is to become thoroughly infused with the enormous range of models, examples, and advice on good relationships that the Bible offers

Our game, therefore, could not fling in texts which were in reality only distantly related to the subject. Instead it must allow people to discover for themselves how the Bible bears upon this issue. Which entails playing the game one week, exploring the Bible the next.

So that is what you have here — the "Matching game" — only one approach to a profound and eternally relevant subject, but a game that we have found to have poignancy and impact whenever it is played.

In week one the players simulate a hectic round of Saturday nights — the emotional minefield of asking out and being asked out. In week two they leave the minefield and turn their attention to the gold-mine. They explore the Bible and attempt to distil its wisdom into ten commandments for relationships.

Matching game — week one

Time required

Week one: Twenty to forty minutes for game-playing, and about the same time for discussion afterwards.

Week two: Up to one hour for Bible exploration.

Suitable for

You will need between ten and thirty people — older teenagers and perhaps unmarried early twenties. An approximately equal number of girls and boys.

The game allows people to win points by manipulating others or treating them simply as objects. Half the players in the game lose points through loyalty! Not terribly pretty, but it reflects in an exaggerated form some of the conflicts and pressures that the teenager faces — to be seen with someone, to have a steady, to prove self-worth by achieving consecutive conquests.

A game played on this basis needs to be approached very sensitively, so before you decide this game is right for your group read through the box — "Handle with care" — opposite.

Aims

1. To bring into the open the problems of boy/girl relationships, particularly in the teenage and young adult age-group. The game highlights:

■ Rejection

■ The "conquest" approach of some people

■ The "mine all mine" dependency of some people

2. To encourage positive thinking about, and understanding of, the way girls and fellows relate to each other.

Handle with care

We wanted a game on boy/girl relationships as it is a sensitive area for most adolescents, stumbling through the minefield of developing relationships. The game we ended up with doesn't shy away from those sensitivities and this frightens us a bit, to the extent that we considered leaving the game out of the book. We didn't, but we want you to share and understand our worries before you use the game.

1. Adolescence is often a time of considerable self-doubt about one's ability to relate to the opposite sex. This game does not play down those concerns. In fact it highlights them a bit — not in an individual way but enough to make the atmosphere crackle a bit. There have been tears, although not usually, and they may have been therapeutic.

2. We want you to have a firm idea of what you hope to get out of the game. That's why we've written an unusually long introduction explaining the purpose of the game. The game itself does not begin from a Bible base. Its place in your programme of Bible study activities relies entirely on how you approach the following week's Bible exploration.

We would encourage you, therefore, to see this game as a two-session activity. The Bible exploration (pages 74–76) is an indispensable part of the overall objective of developing a biblical perspective on relationships.

3. There is a sub-text or hidden message from the way the game is structured, that those who start off badly-placed in the game will never win a desirable partner. Do *you* believe that? It's what we get from the media. Would it be helpful for your group to openly discuss the point?

4. For any in the group who have constantly failed to build relationships with the opposite sex this game might prove a tense experience. Not necessarily though, and you can help matters by keeping it light.

It's certainly not a game to be played if your group are giggly, tired, are at the end of a long weekend away, or are very uptight about the whole subject.

Feeling nervous about playing it at all? Good. Give it some thought, and if you do play it ensure it is accompanied by sensitive teaching and discussion about relationships in general.

Preparation

1. Each player will be given an arbitrary "value" which will be written very large with a felt-tipped pen on a piece of A4 paper, so that it can be seen the length of the room. This "value" wi'l be pinned to them throughout the game. So get a safety-pin for each player.

Now prepare the pieces of paper as follows. With one exception players will have "value" of 2, 3, or 4, and there should be roughly equal quantities of each. So, for example, a group of twenty would need seven pieces of paper showing "value" 2, six showing "value" 3, and six showing "value" 4. The exact quantities are not important so long as there is a spread of 2s, 3s, and 4s.

The exception is that one male will receive "value" 6.

2. Each player needs to keep their own score. So either provide a pencil and paper for each player, or, and it's more fun this way, use tokens. For example, give each person a full and an empty match box and get them to transfer matches when they win points.

3. Prepare one copy of the box headed "Ps points system and rules" for each of the girls and one copy of the box "Qs points system and rules", for each of the boys (see opposite page).

Briefing

1. A long time ago, on another planet, round another sun, in a parallel universe, there were problems. The boys and girls — only they weren't called boys and girls, they were called Ps and Qs — had an amazing way of choosing partners, which wasn't working very well.

2. This game recreates their peculiar method. The aim is to win the game by getting as many points as possible.

3. The game is played in five-minute sessions, because that's how long a week lasted on this planet; just five minutes. Then it's Saturday. You'll know it's Saturday because I'll blow a whistle.

4. You win points by being paired-off when Saturday comes round. During the five-minute week, you'll be buzzing round trying to arrange this.

5. On this planet everybody wore a "value" pinned to their cosmic sky-suit. Some were high "value", some low "value" — though no one knew why — and it didn't really matter except when it came to Saturday night!

(Give out the "value" placards now, by presenting them like a pack of cards face down. *The choice must be seen to be random* — i.e. *you are not allocating "values" to particular people.* However, you do need to ensure an even spread of "values" across both sexes. To achieve this you could arrange the "values" in ascending order, and give them out alternately to a girl and boy. The only exception to the randomness is "value" 6. This should go to a boy.)

Ps points system and rules   KEEP THIS SECRET

1. *If you spend Saturday with a Q* you win as many points as his "value". For example if he has "value" 3, you win three points.

But *if this is the first time in the whole game that you have spent Saturday with him* then you double the points. So if he has "value" 3 then you earn six points.

2. *When you ask a Q to spend Saturday with you* you lose one point, whatever their reply.

Unless it's the same Q you spent last Saturday with. Then you don't take a point off.

3. *Giving away points.* If a Q wants to give you some points, then that's O.K. If you want to give away some points to a Q, then that's O.K. too.

Qs points system and rules   KEEP THIS SECRET

1. *If you spend Saturday with a P* you win as many points as her "value". For example if she has "value" 3, you win three points.

But *if it is the same P you spent last Saturday with* then you double the points. So if she has "value" 3 then you earn six points.

2. *When a P asks to spend Saturday with you*, you win one point, whatever your reply.

Unless it's the same P you spent last Saturday with. Then you don't win a point.

3. *Giving away points.* If a P wants to give you some points, then that's O.K. If you want to give away some points to a P, then that's O.K. too.

6. Girls play Ps, and boys Qs.

7. **How do you win points?** Well this is slightly different for Ps and Qs. And it's important that you keep your points system secret. One good way of spoiling the game is to let out the secret of how you win points. How you win points is explained on this paper. You keep your own tally, so you must be able to understand how the points system works.

(Now hand out your copies of the points system. N.B. It's almost essential to separate the sexes for a few minutes in different rooms while you explain points system.)

8. On this planet it's customary for Qs to stand around the edge of the room, looking pretty. Ps then swagger up to the Qs. The P asks simply "Saturday?" to which the Q replies "yes" or "no". No other conversation is allowed, except to offer to give away points. Ps or Qs disobeying this rule are turned into anti-matter. If more than one P is waiting to speak to a Q, you must form an orderly . . . queue!

9. One thing you may wonder. If a Q agrees to go out with a P next Saturday then can he change his mind before Saturday? Well that depends on you . . .

10. Everyone starts the game with 5 points, whatever "value" they have pinned to their cosmic sky-suit.

Playing the game

Play the game for between four and seven sessions.
   At the end, count up scores to see who is the winner.

Variations

1. The rules are designed "the wrong way round" — girls are given rules that could have been expected to apply to boys, and vice versa. E.g. it is the girls who do the asking out. This deliberately makes for more fun, and keeps the atmosphere light. The game has been played, however, with boys playing Ps and girls Qs, with good results, even if a little heavier.

2. Mature groups could cope with one or two people having "value" zero.

Debriefing

What happened?

1. Who won? Who lost badly? Did the losers feel they had a chance of winning? What did that feel like?

2. Did you enjoy the experience of having a "value" pinned to you or not? Why?

3. Were any of you left without a partner for a lot of the game? Even though it was just a game, was that a peculiar experience? Did that make you want to give up?

4. Ps — was it difficult to ask someone out? Would you have preferred to be a Q? Why? Qs — did you feel like you were being treated as a person or as an object? Would you have preferred to be a P? Why?

5. Did any long-term relationships develop? How? Did this shut others out? Did the long-term couple ever feel they might have been winning more points elsewhere?

What can we learn?

Or: How much does this game reflect real life?

1. In what ways is life on the planet similar to the way we go about finding partners today?

2. How well did people work out the rules the opposite sex were playing under? In real life are girls and boys trying to "win points" in different ways? Does everyone know how everyone else "wins points"? What sort of points are there?

3. What do you think the first rule—see your points system—was getting at? Why the difference between Ps and Qs for that rule? Is it a true difference?

4. Does it really cost something to ask someone out? What? Is that good or bad?

5. The designer of the game wanted rule 3—see your points system—to stand for lots of things. What was the effect of rule 3?

6. Is it true that people's "value" is fixed?

7. Next week we will look at some of the Bible's teaching on relationships. As a result of playing this game is there any piece of advice you would now like to offer your fellow group members?

(N.B. Make a list of any points, to discuss next week.)

Matching game — week two

How you fit this game into a balanced youth-group programme exploring boy-girl relationships is obviously going to be decided by the ages, sexual mix, and experience of your group. This section is intended to help you move from the experience of playing the "Matching game", to establishing some biblical guidelines for teenage relationships.

This activity should not be used at the same session as the "Matching game". If you have debriefed that adequately you will have no time left, anyway. This activity should take place the following week.

Time required

Up to one hour.

Aims

1. To distil from the Bible's assumptions, examples, and teaching, some practical principles for today's boy/girl relationships.

2. To explore, in four small groups, one Bible passage which provides some precedents for how we view or conduct our relationships. The group then use that passage and their own experience — particularly that of playing the "Matching game" — to draw up five practical commandments or characteristics of good boy/girl relationships.

Preparation

Each of the four groups will need copies of the cards below. N.B. You may wish to substitute different passages. If you do, then remember you will need to change the headline, the introduction, and the questions as well!

Group 1
HEADLINE: FOLLOW CHRIST RATHER THAN FASHION
Passage: John 13.1–9

In this passage Jesus shows a model of relationships very different from what many people today search for. Jesus shows that relationships are about giving, not getting.

But what does that mean in practice? From this passage and from your own experience draw up five practical commandments which would help us to follow Christ's example, and be more giving in our relationships with girlfriends and boyfriends.

Write each commandment on a separate piece of paper.

Group 2
HEADLINE: VALUE OTHER PEOPLE AS GOD VALUES THEM
Passage: Romans 12.1–13

This is a passage in which Paul gives some instruction on how we are to relate to other Christians. But we can also apply those instructions to other relationships and particularly to boy/girl relationships.

Using this passage and your own experience draw up five practical commandments which would help us to show by our approach to our relationships that we value other people as God values them.

Write each commandment on a separate sheet of paper.

Group 3
HEADLINE: YOU'RE ON SHOW
Passage: Matthew 5.13–16

In this passage we see an important principle of Jesus' teaching that applies to every aspect of Christian life, not just our relationships. That what we do and how we live can show to the world what God is like.

How might this important principle affect the way we conduct our relationships with boyfriends/girlfriends? From this passage and from others that you can think of, draw up a list of five commandments for boyfriend/girlfriend relationships that would help the world to see God reflected through that relationship.

Write each commandment on a separate sheet of paper.

> *Group 4*
> HEADLINE: GOOD RELATIONSHIPS ARE GOD'S IDEA
> Passage: Genesis 2.18–25
>
> This passage goes right back to basics — God's very first idea for how good relationships can be.
>
> Using this passage and others that you can think of, draw up a list of five characteristics of a good relationship.
>
> Write each characteristic on a separate sheet of paper.

Phase 1

If the composition of your group allows it, split into two groups of girls, and two groups of boys. If, for any reason that split is not possible, don't worry, a mixed-sex group will manage just as well, though you might not get so interesting a variety of "commandments" emerging from the small groups.

Give each group one of the passages above.

Stress that it's up to them to choose what, of the data they have been given, is important. There are no "right answers" at this stage. We are setting out to explore how many different Bible insights might fit together into a whole picture.

(N.B. These do not have to be commandments in the "thou shalt" sense. "The ten commandments" in Exodus 20, you could point out, begin with a statement of basic truths about God. Likewise, their commandments could include some statements of basic principles.)

Phase 2

When everyone has finished, get back together as one group. You should have twenty commandments and characteristics, each on a separate sheet of paper.

Mix them all up. Elect a chairperson. That could be you. Now, in not more than thirty minutes, agree which commandments or characteristics to discard, so that you are left with just ten that seem most useful in helping you overcome the pitfalls and problems you encountered in the "Matching game".

People may suggest rewording some of the commandments or characteristics. This is fine if everyone agrees.

(N.B. To guarantee that the chosen commandments are representative and yet not repetitive, you may need to suggest the final aim is seven, six, or even five, commandments.)

8. Money, money, money

"I ask you, God, to let me . . . be neither rich nor poor. So give me only as much food as I need. If I have more, I might say that I do not need you. But if I am poor, I might steal and bring disgrace on my God."
(Proverbs 30.8–9)

Sound economic advice from an age which knew nothing of credit cards, spring sales, or stock exchanges.

Whether we are rich or poor — and by world standards the nations of the West and we who live in them, are incomparably rich — we must watch out. Money can make us greedy, complacent, and even violent. We can't do without it, but every extra pound, dollar, or franc brings with it an extra decision — how do we spend it? And what we decide reflects more clearly what our values are than do the prayers we say in church on a Sunday.

This game aims to explore the complexity of some typical financial decisions. We won't ever be faced by all of them. Some of us may go through life never having to choose between an extra salary and our family life; or between a Bernadetti Bushwhacker and Band Aid. But we all have small decisions to make, and this game attempts to build a biblical scaffolding around those decisions.

Time required

More than one hour.

Suitable for

Adults, students, and members of youth groups who have some spending power.

Aims

1. To see that the Bible can help us in making decisions about money.
2. To try to apply that teaching.
3. To introduce you to a simple, flexible game model — the role-playing interview.

Preparation

Beforehand

There is quite a lot of card-writing to do in this, so you might like to draft in an assistant or delegate it entirely.

1. Buy some 5 × 3" record cards — preferably two different colours.

2. Decide how many of the case-studies you intend to look at — one per five to seven participants is about right.

3. Write out all role-cards, case-study information cards, and Bible-cards for the case-studies you have chosen.

The role-cards are as on pages 81–84.

The case-study information from which you make separate cards is on pages 81–84. Remember to add details that personalize this information for your group—e.g. the name of Alex Smith's church.

The Bible-cards consist of the appropriate Bible reference found at the beginning of each case study, followed by the instruction, "Discover from this passage two practical principles concerning money and how we use it."

Put the role-cards, the case-study information cards, and the Bible-cards on different colours.

4. Think about who will be the "subjects", i.e. those who play the key-roles, who must be fairly sharp-minded and articulate.

5. Get a copy of all case-study information to give to the "subject."

On the night

1. You will need some Bibles.

2. It is important to warn the "subjects", before you start, that they are to have a key-role.

Briefing

Today the subject is money. (Refer to any past teaching on the subject, or any teaching to come.) This game helps to look at how people use money, how money influences our decisions, and what some parts of the Bible have to say about money.

It consists of a series of case-studies. You are going to look at the situation of a number of characters and advise them what you think they ought to do.

Finally, summarize the programme that is to come, explaining what they will be doing at each phase.

Playing the game

Phase 1 — Bible exploration (about 10 minutes)

Split into random groups—(see page 41)—each with up to seven members. At the same time choose the "subjects" — one per group. Take them aside.

Give one of the Bible-cards to each group.

Meanwhile, brief the "subjects" as below, and give them a copy of all the case-study information about them.

Briefing to the "subjects" — i.e. those taking the main key-roles

1. After you have made yourself familiar with your role and situation, you are to "observe" the groups inconspicuously.

2. You are to join your group after they have reached some consensus on what advice to give you. (Probably after twenty minutes deliberation.)

3. When you join the group you are to question them closely. Play devil's advocate to ensure they have considered all aspects of the issue. Don't let them get away with a simplistic or facile piece of advice. Help them to see what the issue looks like from your point of view. Probe to see what they would have done in your situation.

4. Find out on what biblical principles they are basing their advice.

5. After about ten minutes (or more if the game organizer gives longer) you must ask the group to agree about what advice they would like to give you. It doesn't need to be unanimous. And at that stage you must accept it.

Phase 2 — Case-study information (about 10 minutes)

Give each group its case-study information cards. Ensure that groups with passage A get cards for case-study A, etc. And make sure everybody in the group gets at least one card.

The task is to consider all the information they have been given, including the Bible principles they have discovered in the earlier passage, and decide what advice they, as a group, would like to give to their "subject".

Warn them that the "subject" will come and join them in about ten minutes to receive their advice.

Phase 3 (about 10 minutes)

"Subjects" join the appropriate group, following their brief as defined above.

Phase 4

If time allows, repeat the same process with each group taking on a new case-study. On occasions we have halved the time allocated to each phase above, and thus dealt with two case-studies in the time suggested for one. This works well, but it doesn't give the group much time to get into a brand new case-study. And if the first case-study got the group into heavy arguments, those arguments will brood like a cloud over the discussion of the second.

So don't try and cram in a second case-study if you feel that enough has gone in the first to keep you occupied for half-an-hour of debrief. It's up to you to decide what is suitable for your group.

How much information can people cope with?

Why give the case-study information cards to everybody? Two reasons.

First, every person then has something to say to begin his/her contribution to the group discussion. Even if it is only "Well! my card says . . .", it is a help; and the fact that some of the cards don't make much sense on their own can promote good interaction.

Second, there is a problem in games of all sorts as to how to feed in sufficient information to get the game going. Hand people a whole sheet of A4 and they will retire hurt! This way each person has only one piece of information. If the group ever forget it, the owner of that information can keep reminding them.

As a rule of thumb, in feeding in information to individuals at the start of a game, only feed in as much as can be read in thirty seconds.

If you feed in information before the game, you can be bolder. Give people one or two sides of A4 the night before, and they might be able to take it in.

Case-study A

Focuses on the decision of a church whether to spend money on itself or on a "new" church in Zimbabwe with which it has a link.

Bible passage: 2 Chronicles 24.1–14.

Role-card

Rev Alex Smith

Aged 42

Minister of (. . . insert an appropriate church and town . . .). Interested in family-tree research and local history.

NOTE: 1. In addition to his role-card, give Alex a list of all the case-study information, below.

2. Write each item of the case-study information on a separate card. Distribute the cards to the individuals in the group when you reach phase 2.

Case-study information

■ (. . . insert name of church and town . . .) is a very "untidy" church. The interior paintwork is flaking. The carpets are threadbare. The colour-scheme is yucky. The church needs a complete facelift. *But* the structure is quite sound. No building work is necessary.

■ The official estimate for the work required on the church is £24,000. A lot of money, but then it's an awkward job, requiring great skill.

■ The church treasurer confirms that £24,000 is available.

■ You have a strong link with a growing community church in Bulawayo, Zimbabwe. One of your church members, John Evans, was one of the founding members of that church soon after he arrived in Zimbabwe seven years ago.

■ John Evans has written asking for extra financial support to build a new church building for the fast-growing congregation. Anything towards the £100,000 needed will be fantastic.

■ Alex Smith, your minister, has asked you, as his "support" group, to think through this issue and make a recommendation to him. What action will you recommend?

■ You are Alex Smith's "support group". You were set up three years ago, voluntarily, to pray for Alex and his family. You have become more than that, however. Alex often says to the group, "You keep my feet on the ground".

Case-study B

Focuses on the decision of an outstanding young African doctor on whether to return to her home country of Tanzania, or to stay in the "North".

Bible passage: Matthew 19.16–30.

Role-card

Barbara Chagula

Aged 25 — almost finished training as a doctor.

Active participant in student Christian life in London University.

Home country is Tanzania.

NOTE: 1. In addition to her role-card, give Barbara a list of all the case-study information, below.

2. Write each item of the case-study information on a separate card. Distribute the cards to the individuals in the group when you reach phase 2.

Case-study information

■ Barbara has two weeks to go before she has officially finished her training as a student doctor in one of London's leading hospitals. She has received excellent results — the best of her year.

■ Barbara comes from Tanzania — and has been funded throughout her training by the Tanzanian government.

■ She has this morning received confirmation of the post awaiting her on her return to Tanzania. She would be setting up a new "primary health-care programme" which is a crying need in her country. (Primary health care is designed to train local people in how to fight common but often fatal diseases in their area. It is essential where doctors are in such short supply.)

■ She has also been offered a lucrative research post by the World Health Organization in Geneva, doing research into primary health care. This important work may lead to a permanent post at the WHO.

■ Barbara is attracted to the job in Geneva but is aware how addictive the luxurious, expatriate life-style will become. She is worried that she will never return to her home country.

■ You are *her friends* in the Christian fellowship at University. She has asked you to help her decide. What do you think she should do?

Case-study C

Focuses on the decision of a family about whether the mother should take a full-time job.

Bible passages: Proverbs 30.8–9 and Ecclesiastes 5.10–12.

Role-card

Christine Carter

Aged 34

Part-time teacher.

Mother of Jill (10) and Peter (8). Married to Peter, a teacher.

A church member and house-group leader.

NOTE: 1. In addition to her role-card, give Christine a list of all the case-study information, below.

2. Write each item of the case-study information on a separate card. Distribute the cards to the individuals in the group when you reach phase 2.

Case-study information

■ Christine Carter (aged 34) has worked part-time as a teacher, ever since her children Jill (10) and Peter (8) went to school.

■ Christine and her husband Peter (also a teacher) feel they have enough money to get by, but not enough for good holidays, etc.

■ Christine has been asked to go full-time in her job — double the salary.

■ Christine's son Peter has come home from school crying twice this week. He doesn't seem very happy.

■ Christine is told by the Headmaster that if she cannot accept the full-time post they will have to make her redundant to make way for someone who can be full-time. As a part-timer there will be no redundancy pay.

■ As members of *Christine's house-group* she has asked you to think and pray about her situation, and give her some advice. Should she take the job or should she choose some other option which gave more time for her family? Is there any action her husband should consider?

Case-study D

Focuses on one area of personal spending for a teenager.
Bible passage: Matthew 6.24–34.

Role-card

Emma Rogers

Aged 17

Doing catering course at technical college.

Interested in rock-music and Christianity.

NOTE: 1. In addition to her role-card, give Emma a list of all the case-study information, below.

2. Write each item of the case-study information on a separate card. Distribute the cards to the individuals in the group when you reach phase 2.

Case-study information

■ Emma Rogers is doing a catering course at technical college. She is aged 17. She is still supported by her parents, and lives at home.

■ Bernadetti — a leading clothes store — have just introduced a new line of jackets called Bernadetti Bushwhackers. She says "Everyone is buying them", although they cost about £125 a piece.

■ Emma is always telling her parents that Christians should not look out of date. It is a bad witness.

■ Emma has got £150 saved up, for holidays or whatever she wishes to spend it on.

■ A disaster in East Africa has just hit the headlines. They are appealing for immediate aid through the Emergency Appeals Fund.

■ Emma, who feels increasingly concerned with getting her own spending into proportion has discussed with her youth leader whether she should give £25 to the Emergency Fund, and buy her Bushwhacker; whether she should give £25 and not buy her Bushwhacker; or whether she should give £150 to the Fund; or whether there is something else she should do.

■ The youth leader, with Emma's agreement, decided to open it up for group discussion.

■ You are *members of Emma's youth group*. You must decide how you would advise Emma — the subject is "A Bushwhacker, a bowl of rice, or both?" What would you advise?

Variations

The case-studies are only a sample of what could be devised to explore "money".

You might wish to devise case-studies in which other Bible passages have some significance. For instance:

■ Matthew 10.5–10 or Luke 12.32–34 on the life-style of Jesus' disciples
■ Acts 2.43–45 on sharing money and possessions with other Christians

Debriefing (see page 20)

What happened?

Get everyone together to start with. Each "subject" reports on the advice given and the reasons for it, and adds observations on the way the group decided.

Find out what the "subject" wanted the group to say when he/she first thought out the issue.

What can we learn?

The aim here is to explore at least two areas:

1. *The Bible — whether*, and if so *how* the Bible affected the group's advice.

2. *Our own behaviour* — in the same situation would I have done what I was advising the "subject" to do? How are our financial decisions a "reflection" of our values?

You may either stay all together or revert to your original groups for more detailed discussion.

The Bible

1. Did the Bible figure in your advice? Did you think that the chosen passage was helpful? What other passages did you refer to?

2. Even if you know what the Bible says, are you influenced by it? What problems face the Christian trying to be influenced by the Bible on such distinctively modern issues?

3. Did you find it easy to agree on your "two practical principles"? Why/ why not?

Our own behaviour

1. Have you faced this kind of decision? What did you do? Put yourself in the "subject's" shoes. Would you have done what you advised them to do? Be honest.

2. What are the most important financial decisions you have yet had to make in your life? How did you decide? What were important considerations at the time? Would you now like to be able to go back to that decision and change your mind?

3. Do you think you are ever "hypocritical" with regard to money?

4. Look at how your church, and/or members of the group spend their money in an average year. What does that show of what their real values are? How much goes on themselves? How much on others? Should taxes and rates be counted as expenditure on "others"?

5. Is it possible to establish a guideline for how much of our money to give away? In the Old Testament they aimed for one-tenth, and many people still do today. But Jesus commends the widow who "gave all that she had got" (Luke 21.1–4).

Advise or not advise?

Trying out this game with a group of Methodist students, one participant commented, "Whatever happened to non-directive counselling?" The advice given in this game is, to be sure, directive, and this is one reason why the game is "unreal." God forbid we should ever live in a world where no one used their own judgement, but instead relied on a group to tell them what to do and when to do it. Alex Smith does ask for advice, but it is debatable whether in real life we would be sensible to offer it without probing his own views a lot more. So the game is not a model of "how to give advice". Far from it!

Which points to an important consideration for anyone playing or designing games. To make a game playable one usually has to distort or simplify the real world. And sometimes that distortion may be so great as to devalue it. As they play, players may unintentionally pick up a habit that may be less than desirable.

Only you can decide if the distortion or the simplification is so great as to make the game less useful for your group.

As far as this game goes, we find people easily accept the assumption that they have been asked for advice, and must give it. In the debrief, if necessary, we also look at the issue of "what is the best way of getting/giving advice?"

If this is a major problem, however, the game can be recast so that the group become the voices "inside the subject's head".

Background

There are a couple of bits of historical background that may help in discussion:

1. Up to the eighth century BC, i.e. into the time of the prophets and well past the early Old Testament history recorded in the first ten books of the Old Testament, money hardly existed, and trade and barter were a much more important system of exchange.

2. At the time of Jesus, in Palestine, there would have been three types of coinage in circulation:

■ Official Roman coinage (such as Jesus handled in the passage Mark 12.13–17)

■ Provincial coins from Tyre and Sidon

■ Jewish money

Only Jewish coinage was accepted for the purposes of giving at the Temple. As a result, much corruption was associated with changing money. This is what made Jesus so angry in Matthew 21.12–17.

Other issues

For these questions you should certainly be back in your small groups. I am not suggesting that you should discuss all these points. You might not even discuss one. But they have all been talking points on this games previous "outings". It pays to be well prepared.

Case-study A

1. How smart should our place of worship be? How beautiful?

2. It is often difficult for a church to remain "loyal" to a "missionary" it has not seen for years. What can you do to promote better links?

3. We have lots to learn from the vibrant growing churches of the third world. What can we receive from churches overseas?

Case-study B

This was not simply a financial decision. There may well be reasons why one option will lead to greater long-term benefits. All the same, the case-study is angled in such a way that the lures of expatriate life in Geneva are clear.

1. If you're brilliant do you deserve to be rich?

2. What do you owe to the people who have funded your education?

3. Can you live in a rich world/rich environment and not take on the rich world's values?

4. How else can we, as a group, help such health-care programmes?

Case-study C

The quest for money can be very anxiety-provoking. On the other hand, shortage of money is a prime cause of marital stress.

1. Should the husband be offering to give up his job?

2. Even when we have enough money to get by we often feel poor — why is that?

Case-study D

This case-study might appear more trivial than the others. But it is also much more immediate. It is often the vagaries of fashion that most clearly focus the issue of money for teenagers.

1. Should Christians be "(un)fashionable" on principle?

2. Clothes go out of fashion in a year. Why is that?

3. Do men face the same sort of decisions with regard to fashions as women?

4. Taken literally, Jesus' teaching in Matthew 6.24–34 might simply appear silly! What is the balance between relying on God and looking after ourselves?

5. Ten years from now what would you hope to have done with your life?

Other uses

This game model — the role-playing interview — can be used wherever biblical teaching is ambiguous, unpopular, or a cause of disagreement. For example:

■ The role of women in the church

■ Sexual ethics

■ Sunday observance

9. Bits and pieces

You may recall the fury that greeted the London Tate Gallery's purchase of a new sculpture that consisted simply of a pile of builder's bricks arranged as a rectangle. Was it art? Was it beautiful? Was it meaningful?

This game invites you to try your hand at arranging a pile of bricks! The participants use twenty builder's bricks to create a sculpture which reflects their understanding of one of the Apostle Paul's most famous passages — from Ephesians 2.19–22 — in which he likens the church to a building.

The participants are split into four groups — each having a particular special interest or objective which slightly complicates the task. As a result, not only is the game a profound exploration of one of the New Testament's favourite metaphors of the church, but it is also a study of what happens in a large group when four sub-groups each have slightly different objectives — which is itself a common occurrence in the church.

Time required

Around thirty minutes to create the sculpture, and up to thirty minutes for the debriefing.

Suitable for

Groups of no more than twelve–twenty-five members, preferably upper teens and older. It has been used very successfully with adults. They must be capable of some reflection on their own behaviour and appreciating, at least at some level, "abstract" sculpture.

Aims

1. To explore Ephesians 2.19–22.
2. To see how groups with differing objectives can work together.

Preparation

Beforehand

1. Obtain twenty builder's bricks. These come in all textures and colours. If you're going to play this game in a nicely furnished room try to use one of

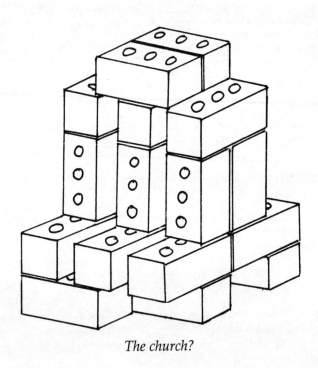

The church?

the least dusty variety — e.g. we've used engineering bricks — the bricks with three circular holes.

2. You might need a plastic or tarpauline floor covering if the bricks are very dusty or dirty.

3. Get a box big enough to hold all the bricks.

4. Make copies of the following Bible passage, notes, and questions for every participant. N.B. We type out the passage as indicated because we find people are able to get into it and see the main ideas more quickly.

(Headline)

> So then, you Gentiles are not
> FOREIGNERS OR STRANGERS
> any longer;
> you are now
> FELLOW-CITIZENS WITH GOD'S PEOPLE
> and
> MEMBERS OF THE FAMILY OF GOD.
>
> You, too, are built upon
> THE FOUNDATION
> laid by the apostles and prophets,
> THE CORNERSTONE
> being
> CHRIST JESUS HIMSELF.
>
> He is the one who
> HOLDS THE WHOLE BUILDING TOGETHER
> and makes it grow into a
> SACRED TEMPLE
> dedicated to the Lord.
>
> In union with him you too are
> BEING BUILT TOGETHER WITH ALL THE OTHERS
> into a place
> WHERE GOD LIVES
> through his Spirit   (Ephesians 2.19–22)

Notes

1. This is written to various Gentile (non-Jewish) Christian churches.

2. The background to the letter is the debate as to whether Gentiles could immediately become Christians, or whether, before they could become Christians they had to become Jews — i.e. be circumcised, and obey all the Jewish laws.

3. "God's people" is a phrase that had previously applied to the Jews, not the Gentiles.

Questions

1. Anything you don't understand in the passage?

2. Are there any phrases which are really important in your opinion?

3. Can you choose a headline which in your opinion (the group's opinion) sums up the passage?

5. Write out the four team's instructions as follows, each on a separate 5 × 3" card.

On one side of every card write the following rules, the same for every group:

Rules

1. The sculpture must reflect your study of Ephesians 2.19–22.
2. All bricks *must* be used.
3. The sculpture is finished *when all participants agree* it is finished.

On the other side, write each group's objectives. You will notice that the first objective is the same for every group. The second is slightly different.

Group A

Objectives:

1. To work with the other groups to create a sculpture.
2. To ensure that the finished sculpture conveys the full meaning of the Bible passage.

Group B

Objectives:

1. To work with the other groups to create a sculpture.
2. To ensure that the finished sculpture is safe — and will not fall down or injure anyone.

Group C

Objectives:

1. To work with the other groups to create a sculpture.
2. To ensure that the finished sculpture is beautiful, attractive, or pleasing to look at.

Group D

Objectives:

1. To work with the other groups to create a sculpture.
2. To ensure that the finished sculpture is finished in the allotted time period.

On the night

1. Decide how to get people into groups (see page 41).

Playing the game

1. Distribute the copies of the Bible passage, notes, and questions, then get someone to read the passage out aloud.

2. Get the participants into four groups.

3. Play a warm-up game if necessary to help build relationships in the small groups—e.g. "Geometry", page 18 or "Arguments", page 19, for older groups.

4. Explain the initial task: **In the next five minutes I want you to read through the passage, discuss it among yourselves using the questions suggested if you wish, and agree a headline — just two or three words — that sums up this passage.**

5. After five minutes reveal the box full of bricks, and hand each group their card showing rules and objectives. N.B. If you want to ensure a thorough examination of the implications of the Bible passage it is important to give the Group A card to a "dynamic" group.

Then explain the next task: **In another five-minutes time I'm going to ask you to join with the other groups in creating a sculpture out of this pile of bricks that reflects your study of the Bible passage. So spend the next five minutes deciding how you, as a group, would like to approach the building of the sculpture. On one side of your card you will see the objectives of your group. The first of these is the same for every group. The second expresses a particular objective that your group should pursue. On the other side of the card you will see the rules for the sculpture. These are, of course, the same for every group.**

Go through the rules as stated on everyone's cards.

6. People should stay in groups for five minutes. After five minutes is up, announce that they have up to twenty minutes to create the sculpture together. You may need to clarify in due course that everybody can be involved in the building of the sculpture — including the clock-watching group D.

7. Observe closely, answer questions if necessary, but in general keep as low a profile as possible. Give a couple of time checks as necessary.

8. Finally, when the sculpture is completed, invite everyone to agree a title for the sculpture.

Variations

1. Any passage at all could be used, though there is an obvious link between builder's bricks and Paul's metaphor of the church as a building.

2. Likewise other building materials could be used. With a small group working in a cramped space you could use Lego. Or you could use

books, chairs, or newspapers. However, choose carefully. We first tried this game with a jigsaw but found that it was not open-ended enough — there is only one solution to a jigsaw. So always use materials that allow many possible shapes.

Debriefing (see page 20)

What happened?

1. Did you find this rewarding/frustrating or both? Why?

2. What did you see your role as? Was it an important role?

3. Which group had most influence on the finished sculpture?

4. Did your opinion get a look in?

5. What are the really important factors in this design?

6. Are you now satisfied with the finished sculpture? If not, what would you have liked to change?

7. What was lost in the process of compromise? Is there anything in your interpretation of the passage that is not in the sculpture? Could it have been got in?

8. Is it still close enough to what you think the passage means for you to "own" the result?

What can we learn?

1. What are the four differing objectives supposed to represent? Are there such differences within your church?

2. What is the effect of having different secondary objectives, even if we share a primary objective?

10. One-hundred-thousand pounds

"Churches need to see and grasp their opportunities." Do you agree?

This "What if . . .?" game forces the participants to think through their priorities for the church. It can be used by itself, but better still as an introduction to further study of the church's role, or as the conclusion to such a discussion.

Time required

Playing time is between one and two hours.

Suitable for

Teenagers and older people with some commitment to the mission of the church. Although designed for fifteen to forty players, it can be adapted for more, taking a little longer to play. It has been used successfully with adults.

Aims

1. To encourage the players to think strategically — "What could our church do if it had the resources?", and indirectly to encourage the setting of priorities. As a side-effect it raises the issues of finance — to what extent is the church handicapped by lack of money?

2. To raise the questions, How can a church set a "biblical agenda"? How does our church interpret the example and words of Jesus into a practical strategy?

3. To expose the problems of groups of people reaching a decision, however well-intentioned they may be.

4. To give a useful example of how a "committee and meeting" game model works.

One-hundred-thousand pounds

The situation

You belong to a thriving church. It is fortunate to own a large building. This building is quite big enough for its current needs.

The building is large enough to take some increase in numbers. It is in very good structural condition. However the hall and rooms badly need redecoration, and so do the toilets and the church kitchen.

The part of the building used for worship has very uncomfortable pews. The organ needs an overhaul.

The church has one minister. He is the only full-time worker for the church. It is generally agreed he is over-worked.

The church relies entirely on the gifts of its members. The income of the church covers the salary of the minister and the general costs of running the church. There is some left over for donations to missionary work and charitable causes.

The town in which the church finds itself is *this* town, with the same problems and opportunities.

The event

An unassuming elderly church member has just died. To everyone's surprise she has left one-hundred-thousand pounds to the church. The will laid down the following conditions:

■ The money must be spent locally; it must not be donated to national or international causes, however worthy

■ The money must be spent on a single project. The project can have a short life-time or be intended to go on for ever

■ The church must decide at the church meeting how to spend the money — the money must be spent in accordance with the words of Jesus, recorded in Matthew 5.13–16 (see over the page).

Apart from these conditions the church is free to spend the money how it wishes — on itself, on needs of the community, or whatever.

The task

Your group must work out in some detail how it would like to use the money. Later there will be a church meeting. One person from your group will present your ideas to the church meeting, and answer questions. Every other group will do the same. There will be discussion and a vote to decide between the ideas. Your idea will be assessed for how well it applies the teaching of Jesus in Matthew 5.13–16, so ensure that you have thoroughly grasped the implications of that passage before you begin your planning.

Preparation

Beforehand

1. On one side of a piece of A4 paper type out the instructions on page 96. If time is pressing, or the photocopier is in paper-chewing mode, it is possible to read the instructions out, but this is less satisfactory.

The instructions may be amended in two ways.

First, for younger teenage groups, reduce the one-hundred-thousand pounds to (say) twenty-thousand. The larger sum seems so overwhelming to this age group that their projects become megalomaniac ("build a sports centre").

Second, adapt the instructions to make the fictional church more, or less, like your church — whichever seems more suitable. The game is played more objectively if there are some points of difference. Furthermore this does avoid the possible embarrassment of implying criticism of the way things are now. The disadvantage is that the fictional church can seem rather unreal, with consequent lack of impact. You must make your own decision, but on the whole, the closer the better.

2. On the other side of the paper photocopy or type out the Bible passage which is mentioned in the old lady's will — Matthew 5.13–16.

You may, if you wish, like to change to another passage. It's a sufficiently surreal idea for almost any passage to be used, but don't make it too obscure, otherwise it won't be taken seriously. You might like to look at Matthew 25.42–45; John 12.2–8 (with a group who are prepared to think about it); Matthew 13.31.

Below the passage put the following questions, or alternative questions which suit your chosen passage:

1. What does it mean for your church to be like salt in your community?

2. What does it mean for your church to be like light in your community?

Get one copy of the instructions and the passage for each participant.

On the night

Gather game instructions and Bible passage (see above), pencils and paper.

Playing the game

1. Split the players into no more than five or six groups. Five is an ideal number of people in a group, seven is more or less the maximum. If at all possible avoid four in a group, as this often leads to two versus two; three people works well. If you have more than about thirty-five or forty people you will need to play a slight variant to the game — see "Variations", below.

2. Hand out the instructions. Allow time for them to be read, and answer any questions. Explain which room each group is in, how long they have (thirty minutes for younger players, rising to sixty for older ones), and where the church meeting will be held.

3. While they are working in groups, go round and check that everyone is happy with their task.

4. The church meeting will need a chairman — preferably a leader, or even the minister! When the players reassemble for the church meeting allow seven minutes for each group to present its ideas and answer questions, followed by at least fifteen minutes of open debate. As people will vote at the end, it is important that they take a note of what each group is suggesting.

5. The matter is put to the vote at the end of the meeting. People cannot vote for their own project. (Question: What if all the groups come back with the same idea? Answer: It's never happened to us, but you would then discuss *why* they've all got the same idea.)

Variations

1. With more than five or six groups (that is, more than thirty-five or forty players) you will find that the presentation of ideas at the church meeting runs on for too long.

To get round this, use larger groups to start with — say ten or twelve people (up to a maximum of twenty). These groups then go away and split themselves into three sub-committees. After fifteen minutes each sub-committee reports back to its group with a raw idea, not worked out at all. The group as a whole then decides between the three sub-committee ideas, and polishes up the one it decides on, ready for presentation to the church meeting.

2. It can be fun to vary the voting system (see box opposite).

3. One other variation suggests itself to an adventurous group, though it has not been tested. Extend the game over two meetings, with a week or fortnight between, to enable groups to do any research they need (for example, the current provision of youth clubs in the area, or average salary for an assistant minister). The groups could then present their idea quite formally, with flip-charts and so on, and might take fifteen or twenty minutes each.

Voting

When a vote is needed there are pitfalls to avoid:

■ Abstention: If it is too easy to abstain, some will fail to consider the choices at hand

■ Crowd-following: In a mass vote, if one lobby is strong, dominant, and articulate, others may duck the choice by voting with the majority

■ Clouding: People must know clearly who/what they are being asked to vote for

■ Anti-climax: After an hour or more of arguing something through, a twenty-second vote can be a real downer. Build-up the voting into a ceremony — string it out a bit — though obviously not to the point of tedium

■ Landslide: Where a game has a built-in possibility that one group will dominate you must avoid that group having a guaranteed majority

So some general rules to follow if you want people to seriously consider the choices, when they vote:

■ Have a written vote, not a show of hands, to discourage abstention and crowd-following

■ Write out the choices clearly on an overhead projector or voting slip, to avoid clouding

■ Have a series of votes. After each vote eliminate the "loser", and run a new vote between the remaining options

■ Try a single transferable vote where there are three or more options — i.e. voters put the three or more choices in an order of preference, then follow two or more rounds of results. Round 1, total up the number of first places of each option. Announce the results. Round 2, eliminate the last placed option, but transfer its votes to whichever option they placed second. Add those second places to the results in round 1. Announce the results. Round 3, repeat round 2, deleting the last-placed options until there are only two options left. This system helps avoid both anti-climax and landslide

Debriefing (see page 20)

- What happened?
- What can we learn?

1. How easily did groups come up with ideas? Is it easy to spend one-hundred-thousand pounds?

2. Is the voting method a good way of choosing between projects? What are the feelings of those groups whose projects did not get chosen? Do they feel that the best one has been chosen, or is it merely everybody's compromise?

3. Is the chosen idea really worth doing? Is it worth one-hundred-thousand pounds? Is it worth trying to raise one-hundred-thousand pounds specially to do it? Does it really apply Jesus' teaching?

4. Was it easy to make decisions about spending someone else's money? Did players feel they were committing future generations or was the project deliberately short-lived?

5. How much money would be needed to do all the really worthwhile projects suggested?

6. Is the chosen idea really the thing that most needs doing in this church?

7. Is lack of money a problem in the church? Why?

8. In this game you had to spend money. What if the game had asked for a "free" project. Is *that* the sort of thing the people of Christ should really be concentrating on?

9. How would you go about ensuring that your project was really of help to the people who were supposed to benefit from it?

11. Roll out the barrel

Christians face three problems when making their minds up about controversial topics. The first is actually reaching a considered, biblical, viewpoint. The second is how to come to terms with the fact that other Christians, also accepting the authority of the Scriptures, have reached a different view. And the third is what to do when a group decision *has* to be made between two viewpoints.

This game explores these problems. In this game a church has to decide quickly whether to allow their over-eighteen youth group to bring alcohol onto the premises. Each person in the game takes on a role, and has to discuss the problem at issue. The game helps the players appreciate that other viewpoints can sensibly exist beside their own, and raises the issue, very starkly, of what to do when people disagree (see box "A note on role-playing"—page 107).

People will use the Bible to support a view, often without exploring the full range of biblical data on the subject. The game thus allows an extra learning point to do with balancing isolated "proof texts" with a more overall view of what the Bible says.

The game is not "fixed ". The results have come out differently every time it has been played — and have included some very ingenious compromises.

This is a detailed example of a classic type of role-playing game, the so-called "Meeting game". It's got three great strengths.

First, it works well. — It is great fun to play, and always provokes a great deal of discussion.

Second, unlike some meeting games, this one arranges for the characters to meet first in pairs, then in groups of six or seven, and finally (as is common in this type of game) in a single large meeting. The advantage of meeting first in pairs, then in small groups, is that in these smaller groups everyone has a chance to express *their* viewpoint and develop *their* ideas and character. The disadvantage is that *we* have had to be very ingenious in arranging sets of cards to fit any number of players between twenty-four and sixty-four, and that means *you* will need to take some trouble to hand out the right cards. But it's worth it.

Finally, this game is a good model for developing your own meeting games (see box "Meeting games".)

One word — the game is set up with a reasonably middle-class church, identifiable as Baptist, and with a fair number of white-collar workers. It's like that because it turned out like that — but there's no reason why you shouldn't modify the characters to reflect any social or ethnic mix you wish, or to create a church of particular denomination, with stewards or P.C.C. members to replace the deacons, etc.

101

Time required

Playing time, including instructions, is usually between sixty and one hundred minutes. Add at least thirty minutes, possibly forty-five, for debriefing.

Suitable for

The game is suitable for any reasonably mature group. For obvious reasons it works well with an all-age group, including adults. You do not need equal numbers of boys and girls. But:

■ You cannot play unless you have twelve or more boys *and* twelve or more girls *and* someone else to be the church meeting leader

■ You cannot play if you have more than sixty-six people, including the church meeting leader

■ You cannot play if the number of boys exceeds the number of girls (or vice versa) by more than eleven

CARE! It's virtually impossible to include latecomers effectively although they can join in the final church meeting, being given any spare cards.

Aims

1. To encourage thought about a particular issue, and allow players to try and persuade others of their viewpoint, whilst forcing them to realize that there is a whole range of sensible, considered opinion.

2. To expose the complications which can arise when a large body of people have to reach a contended decision.

3. To raise the question, how do we reach a view of what the Bible says about a subject?

Meeting games

This is a grandaddy of a meeting game — it took a long time to write and has a lot going on.

Meeting games don't have to be like that. Successful meeting games can go straight to the main meeting, building on:

■ Simple cards showing name, age, and position

■ A briefing sheet which everyone gets, listing personnel and their basic stance, and giving the background to the meeting

Preparation

Beforehand

Preparation is a little time-consuming.

1. You will need a set of role-cards. Photocopy the ones on page 111–118 and cut them up. Put all the "A" cards (the letter is on the top left of the card) in one envelope, the "B" cards in another, and so on — this is so you can get at each type of card quickly.

2. Photocopy the list of church members (on page 119) — enough copies for each player to have one.

3. Decide who is going to play the part of the minister. This should be a mature, authoritative individual. Let her or him know and, if possible, pass on the instructions in advance.

4. Buy some large sticky labels, one per participant. These will be used for character identification.

On the night

1. Provide some felt-tipped pens for writing on the sticky labels.

2. You will need a room large enough for everyone to meet comfortably, and a number of separate spaces for the smaller meetings to take place. Stock each smaller space with a Bible or two.

Playing the game

Start with a short warm-up. Then explain the game as follows.

Briefing

1. For about an hour we're going to play a simulation game as a group.

2. The idea of the game is that everyone in the room will be a character at a church meeting where they have a very controversial decision to make. Each of your characters has a view on the matter and there is no pre-arranged outcome — anybody can say what they like, when they like, and we'll see how the vote goes at the end. The idea is for you to listen to people's views, and to try and persuade them of your character's own views. When the game has been played before, the vote has gone a whole variety of different ways.

3. Let me explain the game. There's a lot to get through — when I get to the end there'll be a chance for questions.

4. Each of us here is a member of Endwood Church. The burning question which is causing a tremendous amount of discussion at Endwood is that the over-eighteen group have asked to have alcohol at their party in a few weeks time. They have a party every year, but they have never had alcohol

before. There is no church rule to cover this situation, so the church has called a special meeting to discuss the problem and make up its mind.

5. In a moment I'm going to give everyone in the room a card, which tells them something about the character they've got to play. But before I do that I want to tell you something about the game and how we'll play it. It's played in three sessions: the first lasts around five minutes, and during this session you'll be in pairs. You'll know who to be with because it tells you on your card. For example, you might be with the person playing your mother, or so on. During this five minutes you'll discuss the issue of drink at the over-eighteen party and find out what the other person thinks. You might even try and persuade them of what you think!

6. At the end of five minutes no bell will go, and no gong will chime — just judge the time roughly for yourself — and go to the second session. Once again the card will tell you who you are with for the second session. You might be a deacon — a church leader — at a meeting of deacons; or you might be at a house-group, discussing the issue informally in someone's home. Or it might be one of a number of other groups. The session lasts about twenty-five minutes. I will come round and tell you when you are nearing the end of that session and your group leader will keep an eye on the time.

7. So that's the first two sessions — first in pairs, then in larger groups. Five minutes, and twenty-five. The third and last session is the church meeting. All together. Anyone who wants to will have a chance to speak and put their point of view. The minister will be chairing the meeting and will end up asking for a vote. That session could last any time — usually between thirty and fifty minutes.

8. We're going to hand out the cards now. It's important that we use the right cards for the exact number of people here, so this will take a few minutes.

Instructions for handing out cards

This is a bit fiddly — please follow the instructions carefully. It's fiddly because it's got to cope with *any* combination of males and females. *But* it's worth the effort.

1. Hand out the David Andrews' card to the person playing the minister, if you haven't already done so.

2. Hand out all twenty-four of the **A** cards. This provides cards for twelve males and twelve females.

YOU MAY NOW FIND that everyone has a card — in which case, well done, you've finished!

OR YOU MAY FIND that you've got exactly one person left without a card, in which case go to instruction 9.

BUT MOST LIKELY you'll have more than one person left, in which case go to instruction 3.

3. IF YOU'VE GOT LEFT <u>BOTH</u> four males (or more than four) <u>AND</u> four females (or more than four) go to instruction 4. OTHERWISE go to instruction 5.

4. Hand out cards according to the table below, then go to instruction 5.

(Note: packs B, C, and D, when used, are used in their entirety. *Don't split them.* Use the whole of each pack indicated in the table. Each contains four "male" cards and four "female" cards.)

		Number of males left		
		4 to 7	8 to 11	12 or more
Number of females	4 to 7	B	B	B
left	8 to 11	B	B & C	B & C
	12 or more	B	B & C	B & C & D

5. IF EVERYONE HAS A CARD then you've finished. If not, then YOU MIGHT HAVE EXACTLY ONE PERSON LEFT — go to instruction 9. OTHERWISE, on to instruction 6.

6. IF THERE ARE seven, or less than seven people left, then move on to instruction 7. OTHERWISE hand out *all* of cards **E**. There are eight of these cards. The names on the cards can apply to either boys or girls. Then move to instruction 7.

7. IF THERE IS JUST ONE PERSON LEFT go to instruction 9. OTHERWISE go to instruction 8.

8. You will be using pack **F**, which is suitable for males and females. IF THERE ARE AN EVEN NUMBER OF PEOPLE, give them cards from pack **F**, starting at card 1, until they all have cards — and you're finished! IF THERE ARE AN ODD NUMBER OF PEOPLE give *all but one of them* cards from pack **F**, starting at card 1. For the last person, still without a card, go to instruction 9.

9. Give the odd person, still without a card, the single card **G** (this card suits a male or a female). That's it!

Well done! On with the game.

Can I say that one good way to spoil the game is to allow other people to see what is written on the front of your card. There's some personal information about your character which it's best if people don't know at this stage. I suggest that when you get your card you don't chat. Read it, and try to imagine the sort of person you are. Try and fill in some of the gaps. You'll need to write your game name in large letters on the piece of sticky paper provided. When you get your card you may find questions arising in your mind — save them for a moment, because I've got some more things to mention, and you may find I answer them.

9. Everyone got their card? O.K. Take your time in reading it. You'll find that in the first session you have to refer back to it quite a lot, but by the time the game ends you'll know yourself pretty well.

10. I expect you've all found at the bottom of the card the name of the person you're with for the first five-minute session, and the second group you're with for the twenty-five-minute session. Just occasionally it happens that the wrong cards are given out and you can't find your partner for the first session — if that happens to you it's a pity but not a disaster. Just hang around for the first session and join in the second.

11. You may wonder if you'll ever be able to find your partner for the first session — you will! — just by walking around shouting — it usually takes less than a minute.

12. You'll need to know where the various groups are meeting for the second session. I'll tell you now:

Deacons in . . .

House-group 1 . . .

Sunday-school leaders' meeting in . . .

Mr and Mrs James in . . .

Over-eighteen group (Antony Mason) in . . .

(House-groups 2, 3, 4)* in . . .

Chair-arrangers — actually do put chairs out*!

* These only meet if the number of people is fairly large and you are handing out a large number of cards.

13. In every room you will find there are a couple of Bibles available, to help you in your task of reaching a considered biblical viewpoint on the issue.

14. Before you ask your questions could I just say a couple of more things. We're not looking for *acting* — in fact putting on accents, or walking like a very old person rather spoils the game because it is so artificial. The idea is to put yourself in someone else's shoes, to try and think like they'd think, and then to explain their point of view.

15. As we're not professionals it can be hard to keep a character for forty-five minutes or more, though the other groups who have played the game have managed very well. If you find yourself corpsing — a word used by actors to mean slipping out of the part and perhaps smiling or giggling — don't let it worry you. Don't make a big thing of it. Relax out of the game for a few seconds, don't put others off, and then join in again when you feel ready. Above all don't over-act! But do stay in character all the time, even in gaps between sessions.

A note on role-playing

Role-playing can be used for two purposes. One is to help people practise a situation they will actually have to face, (or, less commonly, to help them come to terms with something that has already happened). For example, someone going for a job interview will gain a lot from role-playing it beforehand, if feedback is given.

The other use is to put a person in someone else's shoes, to give them some insight into why and how they react. So with teenagers it's useful to get them to role-play the worried mother, waiting up late for their arrival home. What happens is that the pressures on the mother, and the reasons for her concern, become more real, and therefore more understandable to the teenager. This is worthwhile in itself, but becomes even more so if the understanding leads to resolve, or better communication. This is the type of role-play used in this game.

However, in this game we've taken it a bit further. Many of the players are invited to take on board not just the *pressures* on someone, but also some of their *beliefs* about alcohol. There's evidence that in these circumstances people become less antagonistic to views that they did not previously hold.

A good thing in this game, no doubt. But be careful, you shepherds — don't use this approach with *crucial* issues of doctrine unless you are sure of the maturity of your flock.

And another thing. We think in this game we've pushed to the limit the use of the idea that people's beliefs can be derived from their life history. Dangerous that, if taken too far. Think about it.

16. It's great fun to play and you may find it's making you think — but one thing you are not doing during the game is saying what you, as a real person, *actually* think.

17. Any questions? O.K. enjoy yourselves, stay in character, and don't over-act.

Further private instruction to person playing the minister

■ You may be alone for the first session, or Sam Walker may come up to you — this depends on the exact number of people playing.

■ At the church meeting keep a tight reign, especially with young or tired groups. People can sometimes overdo it. Remind them that this is a serious and formal meeting.

■ The church meeting *must* reach a conclusion. You will have to use your own judgement when to bring it to a close. It's better to finish too soon than to let it drift on.

■ Some characters have got a "prompt" on their role-card, which reminds them of some Bible passages which deal with alcohol. One of the tasks at the church meeting is to ensure that whenever a "proof text" is introduced the meeting tries to place this in an overall view of the Bible's teaching on this subject. To help prepare, see the box below, and on page 121.

Your role

From now on the game more or less plays itself. You could take on the role of church caretaker, as you wander round about five minutes before the end of the twenty-five minute session and warn that the church meeting proper starts soon. Just before the church meeting begins, give each member a copy of the list of church members.

Also, arrange with the person playing the minister some secret signal you can give, indicating that he should draw the meeting to a close — you may well detect tiredness before he does.

With a young group you may find that the formality of a church meeting is a surprise — it does no harm to explain this just before the meeting starts.

Note particularly the arguments from the Bible that are introduced at the meeting. Do people simply fling texts around? Or do they see those texts in their context, and attempt to discover biblical principles? Your observations will be very useful at the debrief.

The Bible and. . .

The Bible and alcohol, the Bible and dancing, the Bible and worship, the Bible and birth-control, the Bible and smoking, the Bible and cremation, the Bible and whistling in church. . .

For these sorts of issue there is no easy Bible passage which expresses, clearly and definitely, God's way for his people.

The question is, how should Christians go about making their minds up on an issue? And especially (as in this game), how should a *church* decide what is right?

You must start by asking, "Is it quite clear from the Bible that this matter is essential for a true understanding of God's saving work?" For example, if a church insisted that all men wore ties, then this would be a clear travesty of the gospel, and one should have nothing to do with it.

But if the matter is not vital to faith or morals — and, thank God, that sort of worry doesn't arise very often — we think it might be helpful to go through the following steps. And if you've got the time, don't rush. One sensible solution in the game is to say, "No

---

change this year, we'll think about it during the coming year".

First, read Romans 14 and 1 Corinthians 8 and 10.

Second, what exactly is the problem? In the game, for example, we have four separate things to think through, and muddling them up merely muddles you up:

- Alcohol in general
- Alcohol and youth at a church function
- Sacred premises
- Church public image

Third, what does the Bible say about this problem? (How do you find that out? Get some books on the subject with opposing viewpoints.) You might decide that in the case of alcohol, the Bible:

- Heartily condemns drunkenness (see, for example, Proverbs 23.29–35)

- Has some warning remarks about the risks of alcohol

- Regards it as a natural part of celebration (e.g. Jesus at the Canaan wedding)

Finally, over the years, what has the church said about the problem? Not just your denomination, but the church universal.

After these four steps there will probably be room for honest disagreement. For individuals this may not matter too much — for example some will abstain from alcohol, others will use it for celebrations. But disagreement about how the *church* should act can only be resolved by an act of leadership, taken in the way which that particular assembly of Christians find normal. This will mean that some member of that group might find their church taking a more strict or less strict line than they would have liked.

Let's not fiddle while Rome burns. Don't forget that the early Baptist churches nearly split over whether whole congregations should sing hymns, or just those with beautiful voices, as soloists. Can you imagine justifying *that* to your youth group?

109

Creating role-cards

Creating role-cards that say enough to get people into a character, yet which leave some room for personal interpretation, is a fine art. And what is right for one group may be wrong for another.

So to help everyone see how to create detailed role-cards, we have here reproduced our cards for "Roll out the barrel" in their entirety. You might well think that to create all these from scratch would take you weeks — and you'd probably be right. These role-cards have gradually been refined over the many times this game has been played in the past few years. And you don't need to make them this detailed.

But there are a few things we hope you'll learn from this detailed presentation:

1. Role-cards require care. That doesn't mean every role must be described in as much detail as here. But you can't hurriedly prepare role-cards five minutes before the game starts. In role-play games they are the main data players have to go on, and so they must be right.

2. Role-cards aim to stimulate, not manipulate. In this particular game we want to have a range of opinions on alcohol represented so we have prompted certain characters in a certain direction. But each player works out their own attitudes and arguments consistent with their perception of their character.

3. Role-cards can feed in background information. One of the challenges in a role-play game is to ensure that as each person invents their own character they don't invent two contradictory things. So important pieces of background information can be fed in on the role-card.

4. Prompts on role-cards can help ensure good interaction. On some of these you will see a prompt, e.g. "You find Mr Dodgson rather long-winded". Such "prompts" can help role-play groups to get off to a good start.

Role-cards

Minister David Andrews **Age: 40**

You may take any line you like on this. At the deacons' meeting you must reach a view which the deacons can recommend to the church meeting. At the church meeting you must encourage discussion, after explaining the deacons' recommendation. At the end take a vote.

(Note: at the deacon's meeting watch out for Mrs Dodgson who tries to dominate, and Steven Nash who witters on about nothing.)

Further note: don't start with prayer at either meeting — explain that these items are in the middle of the agenda, and that the meeting started with prayer.

A1 Antony Mason **Age: 28**

Leader of over-eighteen group

The issue of drinking at the party came up by accident, but you're not too sorry as you think it'll give people a chance to re-examine their attitudes. It's only alcoholic punch you're suggesting, and a limited amount of Lager. A lot of your group drink when they go to secular parties. Maybe they'll learn by watching you and your fiancée Kate drinking sensibly. After all, the Bible says that God makes wine to make man happy — Psalm 104.15, if you remember rightly.

Pair: With Kate Vaughan.

Group: Some of the over-eighteen group round for coffee. Encourage them to voice their opinions. Help them to see the opposite view.

A2 John Wright **Age: 26**

Policeman; Sunday-school teacher

You became a non-drinker after a nasty drink-drive accident you had to clear up. You know the Bible says "Wine is a mocker, and beer a brawler; whoever is led astray by them is not wise" (Proverbs 20.1). You are not pushy with your views. You find Mr Dodgson, the Sunday-school superintendent rather long-winded.

Pair: With Michael Field, your flat-mate.

Group: At the Sunday-school leaders' meeting.

A3 Edith Thornton **Age: 60**

Sunday-school teacher, eight to ten years age-group

Parents were total abstainers. You never drink, except Sherry at Christmas.
You don't feel you've missed anything.
You share a flat with Miss Hunt.

You feel it would be unwise to give the seal of approval to alcohol by allowing it on the premises. And the younger ones at the party might not know how to handle alcohol. After all, the Bible says, "Do not get drunk with wine, which will only ruin you; instead, be filled with the Spirit" (Ephesians 5.18).

Pair: With Gladys Hunt.

Group: At the Sunday-school leaders' meeting.

A4 Peter Unwin **Age: 26**

Sunday-school teacher — over-fourteen years age-group

Long standing relationship with Margaret Osbourne — might lead to marriage.

Keen to make your faith attractive to youngsters. Banning alcohol is unnecessary, and may encourage youngsters to experiment just because it's banned — surely better to encourage and demonstrate sensible use. After all, the Bible says, "church helpers . . . must not drink too much wine . . ." (1 Timothy 3.8).

You find Mr Dodgson (the Sunday-school superintendent) well meaning but a bit slow.

Pair: With Margaret Osbourne.

Group: At the Sunday-school leaders' meeting.

A5 Kate Vaughan **Age: 23**

Sunday-school teacher

Engaged to Antony Mason.

You think the issue is unimportant, and could easily get blown out of proportion.
The church should spend more time on major issues. You like Mr Dodgson, the Sunday-school superintendent, but wish he had more drive.

Pair: With Antony Mason.

Group: At the Sunday-school leaders' meeting.

A6 Andrew Renn **Age: 19**

Member of over-eighteen group

Been out at work a few years. Have taken Rosemary Pearce out once or twice, nothing serious. Thinking about asking Jenny Nash out. Over-eighteen group is friendly, and often has good discussions.

Not sure on this issue of alcohol — can see arguments both ways.

Pair: Chatting with Rosemary Pearce.

Group: At coffee at Antony Mason's, the group leader.

A7 Margaret Osbourne **Age: 21**

Yours is a church family. You and Peter Unwin may get engaged soon (you think!). He works in the Sunday-school with young teens, and you're keen to help him — he has a gift for this sort of work.

Nothing wrong with sensible drinking, you think, but not at all right to encourage it on the church premises thus making it an official church activity, any more than you'd show certain films at church which might be O.K. to go and see by yourself. Feel strongly about this — and you enjoy a good argument anyway!

Pair: With Peter Unwin.

Group: Mr and Mrs James (new members) have invited you round for coffee.

| A8 | Rosemary Pearce | Age: 19 |

Keen on Andrew Renn, who has asked you out a couple of times. At the moment, more than anything else, you are hoping he's going to ask you to the party as his official guest.

You couldn't care less whether there is drink at the party or not.

Pair: Chatting to Andrew.

Group: Round at Antony Mason's, youth-group leader, for coffee.

| A9 | Jenny Nash | Age: 21 |

Parents well-known in the church for being teetotal. You are away at college during term, home for holidays now. You have a steady boyfriend at college, though people at home don't know.

A few months ago at college you drank a bit too much at a party, and now you're being careful. Your parents don't know this. This vacation you've made a point of refusing alcohol in a very definite way.

Pair: At Mr Garratt's for a few moments, returning a screwdriver your father borrowed.

Group: At Antony Mason's house for coffee (he is the youth-group leader).

| A10 | Steve Lock | Age: 22 |

Home is a hundred miles away. You are here on six-months' secondment, part of your training. Lodging with Mrs Ives, a motherly type.

You enjoy parties. Can't see any problem with alcohol if you're sensible. A little drink relaxes you. Certainly you've never over-done the drinking.

Pair: Chatting to Mrs Ives.

Group: At house-group 1.

| A11 | Joan Ives | Age: 47 |

You have a lodger, Steve Lock.

You're worried by this issue — your daughter's husband uses alcohol as a pick-me-up, a bit too freely in your opinion, and certainly drank too much when he lost his job. Steve, your young lodger, has come home from parties the worse for wear a couple of times recently, though you've said nothing to him.

Pair: Chatting to Steve Lock.

Group: At house-group 1.

| A12 | Gladys Hunt | Age: 56 |

You like a glass of wine sometimes — often thought how nice it would be to have real wine for communion — after all Jesus turned water to wine. You have a knack of raising a laugh in discussions by recalling funny things that have happened to you or other people.

You go to a lively house-group, though the leader, Mr Garratt, is a little too "smooth" for you.

Pair: Chatting to Edith Thornton, with whom you live.

Group: At house-group 1.

| A13 | Mark James | Age: 33 |

You are a hospital doctor, new to this area and to this church. You are allowed to speak in the church meeting, but not to vote in it. What you've seen of alcoholics, alcohol-caused diseases, and alcohol-caused accidents (about one in ten of road deaths) makes you even less willing to help the drinks' industry by consuming their product or encouraging youngsters to. (There are probably about two thirds of a million alcoholics in this country, and it is a growing problem. Alcohol can cause foetal damage, liver damage, and a weakened heart.)

Although you feel strongly, you don't go around shooting your mouth off.

Pair: With your wife, Patricia James.

Group: In your home, with some church friends you have invited around.

| A14 | Patricia James | Age: 31 |

New to the area, with your husband. New to the church. Can speak, but not vote.

Your new friends don't know that you come from a strict teetotal family, that you broke away and went a bit mad for a while, and now that you've married a man who is a strict teetotaller you don't drink either.

You're worried that your children might go mad like you did, when they're older.

Pair: Chatting to your husband, Mark.

Group: With some new friends you've invited round.

| A15 | Barbara Glover | Age: 45 |

Sunday-school teacher

You are a widow. Your husband died two years ago. You have two children in their mid-teens. At the moment you spend a lot of time thinking and worrying about how the girls will grow up. You have recently made friends with Liz Cole, a career woman with no children.

You enjoy wine, but don't drink much other alcohol.

Pair: With Liz Cole.

Group: At the Sunday-school leaders' meeting.

| A16 | Christopher Garratt | Age: 37 |

House-group leader

Sociable and enjoy company, drink a little, but never drink and drive (well-known for this at work). Keep a full drinks' cupboard, and use it often for friends and business contacts. Only got drunk once (ten years ago) and never again, thank you.

Generally enjoy trying to persuade people of your point of view, though you take a softly-softly approach. If people are taking a point of view without thinking you sometimes take the opposite view just for devilment.

In charge of a house-group which is going well, though you have to watch Miss Hunt a bit, who can wander off the subject.

Pair: Jenny Nash is a student. Chat with her when she returns something you lent to her father.

Group: At house-group 1.

A17　Nigel Bond　Age: 41

Deacon

Became a Christian at the age of 20, and gave up alcohol then. Believe strongly it is better to avoid the risk of leading youngsters astray, especially with alcohol consumption rising so fast (doubled since the sixties).

You are keen to support the minister, David Andrews, in his leadership, though he doesn't always seem to give enough lead. Mrs Dodgson, another deacon, irritates you with the way she assumes that her viewpoint is the only sensible one.

Pair: With your wife.

Group: At the deacons' meeting.

A18　Janet Bond　Age: 37

Deacon

You see nothing wrong with drinking alcohol in moderation. However your husband is teetotal, and although you discuss issues privately you feel strongly that it is wrong to disagree with your husband in public.

You are keen to support the minister, and appreciate his open style of leadership. Mrs Dodgson amuses you because of her very definite views — sometimes, though, you find yourself stung into opposition simply by the self-righteous way she puts things.

Pair: With your husband.

Group: At the deacons' meeting.

A19　Liz Cole　Age: 37

Deacon

You are married to a man who is not a church-goer. You enjoy a career as a micro-computer salesman, and your career is blossoming. You have recently made friends with Mrs Glover, a widow in her mid-forties.

You are firmly in favour of alcohol at the party. The youngsters already drink a bit, there's nothing wrong with it, and you feel the church is somewhat hypocritical about the whole business.

Pair: With Barbara Glover.

Group: At the deacons' meeting.

A20　Ronald Dodgson　Age: 53

Sunday-school superintendent

You are the Sunday-school superintendent, married to Mrs Dodgson, a deacon. You are a fairly quiet person. Your wife is extrovert and forceful. You are not scared to reach decisions, but like to take your time. On this issue you are pulled both ways.

Pair: With your wife.

Group: At the Sunday-school leaders' meeting.

A21　Michael Field　Age: 34

Deacon

You share a flat with John Wright. You are a new deacon. You have decided not to say too much until you have learnt the ropes.

You are open minded on this issue, and hope for a good discussion. On the whole you favour sensible enjoyment of alcohol.
　You like the way the minister (David Andrews) encourages open discussion at deacon's meetings.

Pair: With John Wright.

Group: At the deacons' meeting.

A22　Valerie Dodgson　Age: 51

Deacon

You are married to Ronald Dodgson.

Before the game starts you must decide for yourself whether to be for or against the proposal — but you must be very definite in your views whichever way you decide.

You think that it is always a good idea to state your views clearly. You enjoy a really good argument. You always enjoy deacons' meetings as they lead to quite intense discussion. On this occasion you think the meeting might be evenly divided and you'd like to persuade people of your point of view.

Pair: With your husband.

Group: At the deacons' meeting.

A23　Simon Evans　Age: 44

Deacon

You are not certain about this issue, and you want to be very careful in deciding. Your son is going through a rebellious stage, though you think he'll grow out of it (you've told him this).

In the discussion you hope the minister will give a strong lead, and that he won't let Mrs Dodgson dominate the meeting.

Pair: With your son, Andrew Evans.

Group: At the deacons' meeting.

A24　Andrew Evans　Age: 18

Your dad is a deacon. You row a lot with him. Sometimes he changes his mind, and you can't see the reason. Despite the problems, you basically like him. Although you've wondered about moving out, you can't afford it at the moment.

On this issue you feel the church has got to show its trust of the young people. After all, you have the occasional drink at lunch or after work, and no harm done.

Pair: With your dad, Simon Evans.

Group: Round at Antony Mason's, the youth leader, for coffee.

B1   Rose Dale   **Age: 22**

Sunday-school teacher

You went to college, and got a business studies qualification. You have recently started work in a small company. Your brother Len is a computer programmer, and you think he drinks too much.

You teach the twelve to fourteen range in Sunday school. You *never* drink in your home town or go to local pubs because you think it's a bad example for the children you teach. In your own home, or away on holiday, you'll drink a pint with the best of them — a taste you got at college.

Pair: With your brother Len.

Group: At the Sunday-school leaders' meeting.

B2   Simon Mears   **Age: 32**

House-group 2 leader

Unmarried. Were engaged a few years back, but you broke it off when your fiancée started bossing you. You enjoy your independence. You are an office manager.

You used to drink in a mild way. But last year a college friend was admitted to hospital as an alcoholic — a perfectly normal person, who just seemed to have got hooked on alcohol. This has frightened you. For a six month experimental period you have given up alcohol, though have told no-one.
Your house-group has good discussions, though Edna Dale talks too much.

Pair: Walking to house-group with Penny Gill, a school teacher (unmarried) who lives near you.

Group: At house-group 2.

B3   Leonard Dale   **Age: 22**

Computer programmer, long lunch hours, often in pub with friends. *Very* occasionally have a bit too much.

Sister seems a bit of a hypocrite. She only drinks where people won't see her! Your Dad, Alan Dale, likes Whisky, though not much else. Seems to be drinking more these days.
Your house-group is good, but your mother talks too much when she's there.

Pair: With your sister Rose.

Group: At house-group 2.

B4   Alan Dale   **Age: 47**

You're a machinist at a small engineering works. In three months time you will be made redundant unless orders pick up. You have not told your wife, as you cannot see any point in worrying her unnecessarily.

You like the odd drop of Whisky.
Your wife talks too much at house-group, you think.

Pair: With your wife, Edna.

Group: At house-group 2.

B5   Penny Gill   **Age: 22**

You are a primary-school teacher. You make your own wine. Your boyfriend lives a hundred miles away. You go to a good house-group, though Edna Dale talks too much.

Pair: Walking to house-group with Simon Mears, leader of the house-group.

Group: At house-group 2.

B6   Edna Dale   **Age: 43**

Housewife, married to Alan. Two children, Rose and Len in their early twenties. Your husband has been withdrawn recently, and seems to be having the "odd glass of Whisky" more often than he used to.
You're not shy. You like people. You find you can put them at their ease by chatting away.

You don't see anything wrong with moderate drinking, but you're not too sure about doing it on the church premises.

Pair: With your husband.

Group: At house-group 2.

B7   Steven Nash   **Age: 54**

Solicitor's clerk. Happily married. Two children in their mid-teens, not appearing in this game.

You regard it as important to see both sides of a question. Nothing wrong with drinking — but is doing it on the church premises an encouragement, or a valuable form of training? Your legal experience helps in listing all the points for and against a course of action.

Pair: With your wife Betty.

Group: With Mr and Mrs James, who have invited some friends round.

B8   Betty Nash   **Age: 51**

Part-time accounts supervisor. Happily married to Steven. Two children in their mid-teens, not appearing in this game. Your husband goes on a bit sometimes (you tease him about this), taking himself slightly seriously, but he is good at thinking things through.

You haven't made up your mind about alcohol on the church premises. What are they asking for anyway? Beer? Spirits?

Pair: With your husband.

Group: With Mr and Mrs James, who have invited some people round for coffee.

C1 Hilda Percy	Age: 44

Housewife, mid-forties, three teenage children. Became a Christian three years ago.

Can't understand what all the fuss is about. You are a little worried about Alan Kemp, your next-door-neighbour-but-one. He's 26, made redundant nine months ago, seems to be drifting a bit.

Pair: With Alan Kemp, your next door neighbour.

Group: At house-group 3.

C2 Gordon Lane	Age: 27

Recently qualified accountant. Used to be youth-group leader. Engaged to Pam Hill, a nurse. One of the little jokes you share is when one of you argues strongly for a point of view you don't actually hold.

For this game you may adopt any consistent point of view, and stick to it.

Pair: With Pam Hill.

Group: At house-group 1.

C3 Hilary Lane	Age: 20

Student, lodging with Brian Freeman and his wife.

Teetotal on principle. Believe that Christians should be seen to be different. You enjoy a good discussion.

Pair: With Brian Freeman.

Group: At house-group 2.

C4 Alan Kemp	Age: 23

Living at home, used to drive a van but got fed up and gave it up some months ago. You know Mrs Percy a few doors down, a nice motherly type, but a bit inclined to interfere.

Belong to darts team at local pub. Belong to CAMRA — the campaign for real ale. No beer belly, because you keep fit with the soccer team.

Pair: With Mrs Percy.

Group: At house-group 3.

C5 Pam Hill	Age: 26

Engaged to Gordon Lane, an accountant. You are a trained nurse. One of your's and Gordon's shared jokes is to pretend to argue strongly for something you don't actually believe in.

You drink occasionally. It always intrigues you that moderate drinkers have fewer heart attacks than heavy drinkers *and* total abstainers.

Pair: With Gordon.

Group: At house-group 3.

C6 Brian Freeman	Age: 52

House-group 3 leader

Senior position with firm of insurance brokers. You are very happily married (your wife does not take part in this game). Hilary Lane is lodging with you.

You see moderate drinking as a typical healthy social activity — every society uses alcohol for that purpose, and so did Jesus, even making wine in enormous quantities once when it ran out. Getting drunk once or twice is all part of growing up, and hardly the largest sin.

Your house-group is a good one. Mr Ellis tends to be too definite without thinking things through (your policy here is to encourage others to disagree with what he says) and Pam Hill is a bit quiet and sometimes needs drawing out.

Pair: With Hilary Lane.

Group: At house-group 3.

C7 John Ellis	Age: 68

Grandad, retired. Granddaughter is Georgie Ellis.

You've never drunk. In your day it certainly was not the thing for strict church-goers to drink. You don't see any reason for starting now. After all, communion wine is non-alcoholic in your church! You enjoy house-groups, though you wish people wouldn't challenge the leader so often.

Pair: With granddaughter Georgie.

Group: At house-group 3.

C8 Georgie Ellis	Age: 18

Granddaughter to John Ellis. Still at college. Decided a year ago that you would avoid alcohol, though not to the extent of embarrassing people by refusing wine at meals.

You believe strongly that this is an individual decision — your grandad's strict and unvarying teetotalism you don't really understand, and you want to get to the bottom of it.

Pair: With your grandfather.

Group: At house-group 3.

E1 Francis Armitage	Age: 32

You are married with one child. In the evenings you work in a pub for extra cash.

You have a friend from way back, Robin Bacon, who is teetotal — a running joke between the two of you.

Pair: With Robin Bacon.

Group: At church, helping put the chairs out for the meeting.

E5 Robin Bacon	Age: 31

You work for a meat-tinning factory. You have a friend from way back, Francis Armitage. You are teetotal, Francis isn't. Francis doesn't know that an uncle of yours was killed in a car accident where the driver had been drinking.

Pair: With Francis.

Group: Helping put chairs out at church.

E2 Jo Foster	Age: 21

You and your sister Val live at home with your parents. You're at art college. Val works in an office, doing quite well. Val is older, and sometimes, you think, a bit staid. You suspect that Val will be against drink on the church premises. You are not sure about your own views — you'll probably be for it just to try and stir up some genuine discussion of the issues.

Pair: With Val.

Group: At the youth leader's home for coffee (name: Antony Mason).

E6 Gerrie Cobb	Age: 27

Physiotherapist, in hospital. High proportion of time spent exercising car accident victims. Many of the accidents were caused by alcohol.

You have a friend Leslie Elm, who runs a food hall, which sells alcohol. For this game you may take up any consistent attitude you wish.

Pair: With Leslie.

Group: At church, helping arrange chairs.

E3 Val Foster	Age: 23

You and your sister Jo still live at home with your parents. You are doing well for yourself in an office. Jo is at college and a bit immature — sometimes you enjoy leading Jo on, giving the impression that you're a bit more of a stick in the mud than you actually are — Jo is still quite young and has very fixed views.

You believe that drink on the church premises is one of the most *unimportant* issues that could possibly take up the church's time.

Pair: With Jo.

Group: Helping put chairs out for church meeting — a discussion will develop.

E7 Stevie Ridgway	Age: 30

Married, no children. Your father-in-law brews his own beer, and you're thinking of taking the hobby up.

You feel that the church should take every opportunity to discourage alcohol with youngsters until they are old enough to think sensibly for themselves.

Pair: With an old friend, Kim Pollard.

Group: At house-group 1.

E4 Leslie Elm	Age: 31

You are in charge of the food section of a department store. The food section includes alcohol. Sales of alcohol in your store (and nationally) are increasing steadily.

Your good friend is Gerrie Cobb, a physiotherapist.

Pair: With Gerrie.

Group: Helping put chairs out at church.

E8 Kim Pollard	Age: 32

Married, happily.

You're not too sure what to think about drink in the church. But you're sure it's not a simple decision. You want to think it through very carefully.

Pair: With Stevie Ridgway, an old friend.

Group: Coffee at Mr and Mrs James, who have invited some friends round.

F1	Chris Marks	Age: 32

Sunday-school teacher

Journalist. You drink, and think that hours of discussion about one party is a waste of time. Basically you are prepared to go along with any sensible suggestion.

Pair: With a friend Nicky Herbert.

Group: At the Sunday-school leaders' meeting.

F2	Nicky Herbert	Age: 32

A divorcee. You always had a relaxed attitude to alcohol, but your thirteen-year-old son has recently got in with a bad crowd, and the thought of glue-sniffing and soft-drugs abuse has started to worry you. You have not yet made up your mind about the party — your son won't be old enough to go anyway.

Pair: With an old friend, a journalist, Chris Marks.

Group: At the home of Mr and Mrs James, for coffee.

F3	Clem Graham	Age: 57

Deacon

One of your children is married, the other divorced. Freddie, one of your grandchildren, whose parents are divorced, is staying with you. Freddie is eighteen, rather quiet.

You are more or less teetotal, more from habit than any great conviction. You have not decided how to vote.

Pair: With Freddie.

Group: At the deacons' meeting.

F4	Tony Allen	Age: 37

You are a health and safety at work inspector. You never drink and drive — you know too much about alcohol and machinery and mistakes. Otherwise you can't see any problems with alcohol. Pat (your parents had just two children, you and Pat) you see very little of — Pat tends to dominate discussion, and sometimes seems a bit of a prig.

Pair: With Pat.

Group: At house-group 1.

F5	Pat Allen	Age: 39

Deacon

You are a draughtsman. You like things neat and tidy. This is not at all like Tony (your parents had just two children, you and Tony) who seems sometimes just to muddle through things.

You have already prepared your arguments for the deacon's meeting — and you are looking forward to trying them out on Tony. (For the game your arguments can be either for or against, but must be very definite.)

Pair: With Tony Allen.

Group: At the deacons' meeting.

F6	Freddie Graham	Age: 18

Your parents are divorced. You are on holiday with your grandparent, Clem Graham, whom you like, though you find it hard to discover what Clem really thinks.

You drink at parties, though not much — anyway, you don't go to many parties. You think Clem is teetotal, and will be against the idea of drink at the over-eighteen party.

Pair: With Clem Graham, your grandparent.

Group: At Antony Mason's for coffee (he is the youth leader).

F7	Laurie Wilson	Age: 20

It was your suggestion that alcohol should be served at this year's party — you're on the committee. You've got all the arguments at your fingertips. You are suggesting Lager and a punch.

Your friend Ross thinks you are rocking the boat unnecessarily — things will change slowly anyway.

Pair: With Ross.

Group: At the youth leader's home for coffee (Antony Mason).

F8	Ross White	Age: 20

You are a friend of Laurie Wilson, who put up the whole idea of having alcohol at a party. Personally you think it's not worth having a church row over rather a tiny matter of principle. You notice that Laurie often seems to win arguments; you're determined not to lose this one.

Pair: With Laurie.

Group: At house-group 1.

G1	Sam Walker	Age: 19

Sunday-school teacher

You are a Sunday-school teacher. You started work a year ago, as a catering trainee. Last week you went on a trip organized by the firm for the day to Boulogne in France. You got drunk. You feel terrible about this. Should you carry on Sunday-school teaching? Should you give up drinking?

You are not sure what to make of your Sunday-school superintendent — sometimes he doesn't seem as sure of himself as you'd like.

Pair: See the minister (Mr Andrews) for advice.

Group: At the Sunday-school leaders' meeting.

List of church members

(Not all will be present)
(One copy to be given to every participant — to help you see who's who at the church meeting)

	Age		Age
ALLEN, Pat (Deacon)	39	HUNT, Gladys	56
ALLEN, Tony	37	IVES, Joan	47
ANDREWS, David (Minister)	32	JAMES, Mark	33
ARMITAGE, Francis	32	JAMES, Patricia	31
BACON, Robin	31	JOHNSON, Olive	48
BLANCHARD, Louisa	74	JOHNSON, Valerie	20
BOND, Nigel (Deacon)	41	JOHNSON, David	50
BOND, Janet (Deacon)	37	KEMP, Alan	23
COBB, Gerrie	27	KING, Geoff	25
COLE, Liz (Deacon)	37	LANE, Hilary	20
DALE, Alan	47	LANE, Gordon	27
DALE, Edna	43	LEE, Peter (House-group leader)	41
DALE, Leonard	22	LOCK, Steve	22
DALE, Rose (Sunday-school teacher)	22	MARKS, Chris (Sunday-school teacher)	32
DODGSON, Ronald (Sunday-school superintendant)	53	MASON, Antony (Youth leader)	28
DODGSON, Valerie (Deacon)	51	MEARS, Simon (House-group leader)	32
ELLIS, John	68	NASH, Betty	51
ELLIS, Georgie	18	NASH, Steven	54
ELM, Leslie	31	NASH, Jenny	21
EVANS, Simon (Deacon)	44	OSBOURNE, Margaret	21
EVANS, Andrew	18	PEARCE, Rosemary	19
FIELD, Michael (Deacon)	34	PERCY, Hilda	44
FREEMAN, Brian (House-group leader)	52	POLLARD, Kim	32
FOSTER, Val	23	RENN, Andrew	19
FOSTER, Jo	21	RIDGWAY, Stevie	30
GARRATT, Christopher (House-group leader)	37	THORNTON, Edith (Sunday-school teacher)	60
GILL, Penny	22	UNWIN, Peter (Sunday-school teacher)	26
GLOVER, Barbara (Sunday-school teacher)	45	VAUGHAN, Kate (Sunday-school teacher)	23
GRAHAM, Freddie	18	WALKER, Sam (Sunday-school teacher)	19
GRAHAM, Clem (Deacon)	57	WHITE, Ross	20
HARPER, Heather	25	WILSON, Laurie	20
HARPER, Tony	31	WRIGHT, John (Sunday-school teacher)	26
HERBERT, Nicky	32		
HILL, Pam	26		

Debriefing (see page 20)

What happened?

Almost always this game provokes a lot of natural discussion, and if you have time it is no bad idea to break for coffee when it is finished, and hold the more formal debrief after the coffee.

What can we learn?

1. Did anyone find their own opinions changing, or becoming less certain, as the game went on? What type of arguments were persuasive? What type of people were persuasive — and what type weren't?

2. How interesting was it trying to put yourself in someone else's shoes? How *easy* is it for a person to change their mind? What things make it easier? Harder? Is it a particularly good thing to have an open mind? How often did those with open minds get trodden over by those with strong views?

3. How many groups found themselves following a strong personality without fully considering the facts and arguments?

4. Did arguments from the Bible get a fair airing? Which ones? Are they the only possible arguments? How do you get a picture of the whole Bible's teaching when there are conflicting statements? (see boxes "The Bible and . . ." (page 108) and "Proof texts" opposite.)

5. How suitable is a large group, the size of the church meeting, for discussing these issues? How easy is it to have good discussion in such a group? What better ways are there?

6. How good an idea was it for the youth group to bring matters to a head by asking for Lager at the party? (And when did the fact it was Lager, rather than Spirits, emerge?)

7. Were people unfairly stereotyped?

8. What else was learnt?

Other uses

A role-playing meeting game can be used to discuss any topic, and can be made as simple or as complicated as you like. Make up your own! How about the following:

1. For theologically-minded groups:

■ Changing the way the church does things to allow non-baptized people to take communion

■ Holding a service of marriage for two professing Christians, one of whom is divorced

2. For those interested in social issues and the way the church should respond:

- Showing the anti-nuclear film *War game* in the church hall, as a church activity

- The church, *as a church*, sending an official donation to Life (an anti-abortion agency), or C.N.D., or National Viewers and Listeners Association (the association founded by Mrs Mary Whitehouse), or . . . etc.

Proof texts

As chairman of the meeting you will quickly become fed up with the tendency of one or two characters to fling around proof texts from the Bible to support their view. And part of learning from this game is to see how difficult it is to reach an overall view of what the Bible says on a subject. See, the box "The Bible and . . ." (page 108) for some advice on this subject.

The debriefing could include a discussion on how to handle the proof text habit, in which case the following points are worth noting:

1. We all tend to take texts out of context, and to pretend this is a fault that only the other person has is to forget the log in our own eye. And we do it because we all have difficulty holding together in our memories a very wide range of biblical opinion. We tend, therefore, to remember only the bits that support our viewpoint. We may not think we are being "one-sided" but our selective memory ensures we are. So do not condemn the "text-flinger". Do not drive them into a corner. Instead treat them lovingly and encourage them to listen to those who are trying to present a balanced picture.

2. Have to hand some reference material which allows you to feel confident that an overall biblical picture can be discovered.

3. Sometimes ask the person who produces the proof text to look up that reference in their Bible and tell the meeting in what context that passage was used.

4. If appropriate, have a flip chart or overhead projector on which you can record some of the texts and their context. Show how they balance each other.

Don't allow people to argue simply on the basis of their one text. Encourage them to look at a broader picture. That could be an important learning point for many people.

12. Zac's map

The story of Zacchaeus must be one of the most popular in the New Testament. From Sunday-school upwards it is wheeled out to illustrate anything from "honesty" to "opening your home to strangers". This game gives a new angle. Rather than focusing on Zacchaeus, it focuses instead on Jesus.

Look at Luke 18 and 19 and see the context of the story. Luke places it alongside four other famous and controversial incidents. "The Parable of the Pharisee and the Tax Collector" is followed by "Jesus Blesses Little Children" — which together challenge prevailing religious values that God was only interested in the righteous and the adults. Two further incidents follow, challenging social values. Jesus' hard words to a rich man (18.18–30) leave the crowd gasping, "Who, then, can be saved?" Finally, as Jesus heads for Jericho, he heals a blind beggar — one of society's rejects. Then, enter Zacchaeus.

It is still difficult for us, however, to cross the centuries and appreciate just how unconventional Jesus was. So try out this game, in which the group become a regional committee preparing for a visiting dignitary. Will they plan a Jesus style walkabout?

Time required
About seventy minutes.

Suitable for
Any group which can cope with maps — though the fact that people work in pairs means that only one person per pair needs to understand the map. Very useful also if you are only just beginning to experiment with games, as this one is quite simple.

Aims
1. To explore the story of Zacchaeus.
2. To see how Jesus reverses establishment values.

Preparation

Beforehand

1. Find a simple map of your area, and get photocopies of it for every person in the group. Don't infringe copyright. If you cannot find a suitable map, draw a simple one and photocopy that. The map should show the main features of your town/city/area—and include main street names (but see Variation 2). As always, get a few extra copies as emergency rations—in case Samantha brings six friends to the youth fellowship!

2. Pencils and rubbers will be essential.

3. Get one large brown envelope and one photocopy of the Planning Committee instructions, per two participants.

Playing the game

Warming up

People may not be used to maps, so begin with a simple introduction if necessary. In pairs, mark on the map the place in which they are meeting now, and one other major landmark. Something that they will all have heard of. Finally, mark on the map a route anyone could take to get between these two places.

Briefing

It has been decided that on his forthcoming tour of this country, the Pope (see also Variations) . . . yes the Pope . . . is going to visit our area. Why? Because it is typically (English/Welsh/American/exciting — insert appropriate words) that he just had to come. A Planning Committee has been set up to organize his visit. You have been appointed to submit a draft proposal for the route of one of his famous walkabouts.

He has just one hour, during which he must see what you consider to be the most important people, sites, projects, and communities in this area. It's up to you to decide what you think is important.

The Planning Committee want you to draw your proposed route on your map and mark any place that the Pope will stop, and whom he will see. The Committee will also want to know why you have chosen the places you have chosen.

Phase 1–Planning a route (10 minutes)

It is best if this phase is fairly rushed — because all you want are the immediate thoughts. Using one of their two maps, each pair prepare a route.

Phase 2

Hand each pair an envelope containing the Planning Committee's extra instructions. See below.

Planning Committee instructions

Please reconsider your route in the light of the following story:

Jesus and Zacchaeus

Jesus went on into Jericho and was passing through. [2]There was a chief tax collector there named Zacchaeus, who was rich. [3]He was trying to see who Jesus was, but he was a little man and could not see Jesus because of the crowd. [4]So he ran ahead of the crowd and climbed a sycamore tree to see Jesus, who was going to pass that way. [5]When Jesus came to that place, he looked up and said to Zacchaeus, "Hurry down, Zacchaeus, because I must stay in your house today."

6 Zacchaeus hurried down and welcomed him with great joy. [7]All the people who saw it started grumbling, "This man has gone as a guest to the home of a sinner!"

8 Zacchaeus stood up and said to the Lord, "Listen, sir! I will give half my belongings to the poor, and if I have cheated anyone, I will pay him back four times as much."

9 Jesus said to him, "Salvation has come to this house today, for this man, also, is a descendant of Abraham. [10]The Son of Man came to seek and to save the lost."

(Luke 19.1–10)

The Planning Committee wish it to be known that they think the route for the Pope's walkabout should reflect the same priorities as Jesus showed in this story:

1. An interest in people.

2. An interest in the rejects and sinners.

How will you change your route to comply with this requirement?

Give pairs ten minutes to put their finished routes into the envelope marked with their names, and to discuss and adjust their route.

You now have two options — either:

1. Proceed to the Debriefing, concentrating on the question "How did you change your route as a result of the Zacchaeus story?" Or, much better,

2. Carry on to phase 3 — the Planning Committee's decision as to which route to accept.

Phase 3 — The Planning Committee (20 — 30 minutes)

Chair the committee yourself. All the group are members. Each pair must very quickly present and explain their route, and how it meets the requirements. The Planning Committee must discuss and vote to draw up a short list of three routes. Then, if you wish, culminate with a vote on which of those three shall be accepted.

As chairman, try to constantly refer the discussion back to the Zacchaeus story which is the basis for decision making.

Variations

1. It might pose problems to use "the Pope" — comparing him with Jesus might throw up unfortunate and unnecessary side-issues. So pick another character if you wish, but whoever you choose, ensure that it is a religious not a political figure, and that he/she is important enough for the simulation to be credible — e.g. it would be unlikely that a "visiting preacher" would be given a walkabout, and a massive Planning Committee.

2. Instead of photocopied maps, simply brief each pair to draw their own map showing whatever features they want to show.

This variation is essential if group members are from many different towns and areas. If so, ensure that at the start they pair up with someone from the same area or at least with someone who knows their area. In some instances a pair has even chosen to map a "third" place, known to both of them, but where neither of them live.

If you use this variation, phase 3 becomes a National Planning Committee receiving requests from many different places, towns, or organizations who each wish the Pope to visit them. Each is asked to submit their route which shows that a visit to their town is going to be particularly worthwhile in the terms defined by the Zacchaeus story.

Debriefing (see page 20)

Phase 3 will do away with the need for a long debrief. Many of the issues will have been already discussed, though as always, spend time drawing out what people have learned and how they are feeling.

■ What happened?

■ What can we learn?

1. The route — how did you change your route as a result of the Zacchaeus story?

2. What were you trying to achieve by these changes?

3. What are the differences between various routes?

4. Do you think anyone in the group had a particularly good/bad route?

5. Was is difficult to decide what was important? Why?

13. First things first

There are more than one hundred countries where Bible Societies provide Bibles. Every country has different needs. Some need the Bible in their own language for the first time. Others need help in learning to read it. Others need special help in printing and binding it.

The Bible Societies rely on people like you to support their work, but every year only a few of the many possible projects are taken on because money is always scarce. This game helps everyone understand this situation. It introduces a very complicated subject in a simple way. Each person commits themselves to one Bible project, arguing for the importance of that project in a regional group, then an International Committee. By the end, everyone should realize a little more how rare and precious a Bible is.

As a side issue, this is one of the most adaptable game "models" in this book. It's a structure that you can apply to development, unemployment, indeed any issue that gives rise to "projects" that need money. One-hundred-thousand pounds (page 95) makes different use of the same model.

Time required

Fifty-five minutes for the game. Up to forty-five minutes for the debriefing.

Suitable for

Any large church group (over twenty people) aged sixteen upwards. Some background knowledge of Bible Society helps, which makes it particularly suitable, we find, for adults.

Aims

1. To appreciate the shortage of Bibles in many countries.
2. To place a greater value on our own Bibles.

Preparation

Beforehand

1. Prepare project-cards. Simply photocopy pages 131–134 six times, and cut out the cards. Keep those marked Region A separate from Region B, separate from Region C, etc. Alternatively type out your own versions, because some project-cards might need updating as the world political scene changes.

2. (Optional) Prepare role-cards, one per participant. Write one role from pages 135–137, on each card. Label them Region A, B, or C, etc. Keep those marked Region A separate from Region B, separate from Region C, etc.

3. Prepare "blocker" cards — a card with the following words:

"You are a 'blocker'. The regional group will attempt to reach a unanimous decision. Your role is to block that decision by disagreeing, *until you are satisfied that all issues have been discussed*, or until time runs out. *BUT* do not let on that you are a blocker and do not accept the 'chairpersonship' of the group, if it is offered to you".

4. Recruit assistants to help you on the night, and a panel (phase 3) if you are going to use outsiders.

On the night

1. Count how many players you have and therefore how may regions you will use. This is very important! If the game is to work well there must be between four and ten players per region, therefore the total number of players will determine how many regions you use. For example, twenty-five players could use five regions. The best number is eight per region.

Which regions you use can be determined by the interests of your group, but we are assuming for simplicity that if you want five regions you will use A, B, C, D, and E.

Take all the project-cards and role-cards that apply to the regions you are using, and set aside all other cards — you won't be needing them at all. Take one blocker-card per region, set the others aside.

2. Each region should be allocated its own private area — a corner of a room, or a separate room altogether. Mark this space by sticking up a large letter A, B, C, etc. above it.

3. If you wish, warn your "blockers" they will be having a special role.

Playing the game

Warming up

This is a "persuading game" in which arguments help to crystallize important issues, so start with "Arguments" page 19. N.B. Once the group are in pairs, if there is one person left over recruit them as a "blocker".

Briefing

"You are all good at arguing. No surprise at all. Now you are going to apply your arguing skills to getting your way in the world of the "Allied Bible Societies". You see it is the year (insert next year's date) and money is short as always. Every region of the world has proposed its projects which they think will increase Bible-use in their region, but only a few of those many projects are going to receive the much-needed subsidy. The rest will be rejected. Every project needs the same amount of money, and all the projects are fighting against each other for that valuable subsidy. Who will get it? Well that's up to you."

Phase 1 — Pairs (10 minutes)

1. Hand out the project-cards. Give each pair one card only. You must ensure at this stage that each region has approximately the same number of people, so rather than handing out all the Region A cards followed by all the B, give the first pair A, the second B, etc.

Introduce the task:

"Still in your pairs I want you to decide which *you* think is the most important project. You may disagree, but try to persuade your partner you are right. N.B. All the projects require the same subsidy — they cost the same amount of money!"

2. (Optional) After three minutes, hand out the role-cards. Each person should be given one card — from the same region as their project-card.

Introduce the task:

"This card indicates your role for the rest of this game. Think of that person. What would they be likely to support? Now, in role, agree with your partner in what order of priority the projects should be. You must agree!"

Phase 2 — Regional groups (20 minutes)

1. After the pairs have finished, or when the allotted time has been allowed, announce the next phase. Announce where each regional group will meet, but before people go, announce the tasks.

"You must now make your way to your regional areas. In your regional groups you have two tasks: 1. elect a chairperson for your meeting, and 2. unanimously agree which of the three regional projects you are going to put forward to the International Committee. Which of these projects do you think will most benefit the Bible-cause in your region?"

2. Recruit your blockers. One per region. Inconspicuously hand them a blocker-card as they make their way to the regional group. They should be reasonably articulate, assertive, and persuasive, because it is their role to

ensure that all possibilities are considered. You might like to have warned your blockers in advance.

3. Watch how the groups behave and help them if they have difficulty understanding the task. Towards the end of the time give a time-check and remind them to appoint a spokesperson to present their case.

Phase 3 — The International Committee (25 minutes)

Everyone gets back together in plenary, and each region presents its chosen project to a panel. This panel can be made up of either:

■ Your assistant plus the blockers from each region, or better still

■ A specially recruited team of outsiders who are only introduced at this point, having been hidden in the kitchen so far!

After all the projects have been presented, the panel, or anyone else, asks questions about each project, to clarify it. Then the panel vote on which project to accept, and which to put second as a "reserve".

The panel's decision must be *unanimous*.

If you use less than eight regions you can explain the absence of the other regions from the International Committee as the result of a boycott, a political coup, delayed transportation, etc.

Variations

1. The game can be played without roles. This simplifies phase 1, but cuts down what you can learn from the game.

2. We have said that all projects need the same subsidy. This game has been played, however, with many different projects of different values, and an overall budget limit.

Debriefing (see page 20)

■ What happened?
■ What can we learn?

About the projects:

1. Were any of them particularly interesting?
2. Were any of them particularly irrelevant?
3. Did the best get chosen?
4. Did any of you feel your project was badly treated? Why?
5. What more did you want to know about your project?

About your choices:

1. How did you decide what was important?

2. Did you have to compromise?

3. Who, or what arguments were most convincing?

4. Was there any agreement that, for example, a first-time Bible was better than a New Testament, which was better than a selection? Why?

■ What do we do next?

Explore any country or project that particularly interested your group, and do what you can to assist the much-needed work of the Bible Society in your area and all around the world.

Breakaway

The most notable occasion we played this game was with a real live collection of Bible Society staff. All one hundred of them. They bickered and battered their way to a standstill in most of the regional groups, yet still managed to arrive at a priority project. Feeling ran so high, however, that one group set up a breakaway Bible Society. Repercussions were still ringing around the office two months later.

Which proves a point! The success of a simulation is often dependent on how much background knowledge your group have of the subject before they start. The more the better. Simulations reinforce or harness knowledge better than they teach it from scratch. In practice this means that simulations are best played as part of a general education programme on a given subject rather than as one-off exercises.

Project-cards

Region A — Latin America

1. Argentina

A stall at the internationally famous Argentine bookfair. Thousands of people visit the fair — including many influential in society. Sales in past years have been encouraging.

2. El Salvador

Scriptures for a mass visitation called "Urban Operation" in the country's six main cities. Members of fifty-two churches will visit the entire community in each city!

3. Bolivia

The Bible Society wishes to modernize its worn stock of the well-known biblical film series "Cathedral Films". These films are shown in Bible Society's three main centres.

Region B — The Muslim world

1. Algeria

Rent for the only Christian bookshop in North Africa. This shop is both a symbol of Christian presence, and a centre for distributing Bibles.

2. Egypt

Selections (selected Bible passages printed in a leaflet) for children and students. These selections would be in Arabic, to aid outreach among the young.

3. Turkey

Purchase of space at two annual trade fairs (in Ankara and Ismir), and four regional book fairs, *and* printing 20,000 Scripture calendars to be given away at these fairs.

Region C — British Isles

1. *England*

Evangelistic Scripture selections for housewives. These leaflets would be given to them by church visitors. The subsidy would provide 100,000 eight-page leaflets.

2. *Wales*

Translation of the Bible into modern Welsh. Spoken by half-a-million people out of a population of two-and-a-half million people.

3. *U.K.*

Scripture leaflets for gypsies. Giving the same text in English and their own language, Romany. Fifty thousand leaflets would be translated and produced with the subsidy.

Region D — The communist world

1. *People's Republic of China*

Provision of a Bible printing-press for Chinese scriptures.

2. *Soviet Union*

Nineteen thousand New Testaments for Western Armenia. This is a project that should have been funded last year, but money was not available.

3. *Poland*

The subsidy would buy some of the paper for printing 65,000 Polish Bibles — paper is very short in Poland, and must be paid for and imported from elsewhere in Europe.

Region E — Central and Southern Africa

1. Sudan

Part of the cost of a new Bible Society headquarters building in Juba — South Sudan. A building-plot is available, but if they don't build soon the government will take it over. Cheap experienced builder is available.

2. Zimbabwe

New Testaments for refugees returning to their homeland — many of whom had been forced to burn their Bibles in the civil war. Forty-five thousand New Testaments in the refugees' own languages.

3. Rwanda

Most people in Rwanda can speak Kinyarwanda, but the Bible is one of the few books available in the language. Bible Society wish to provide 7,000 complete Bibles.

Region F — South East Asia

1. Indonesia

1,150,000 Scripture booklets for people learning to read. These new booklets are more advanced than those used in the already successful New Reader Programme.

2. Bangladesh

A New Testament for Bengali Muslims. 20,000 copies are to be subsidized so that the local people can afford to buy one. This translation uses terms particularly familiar to Muslims.

3. Vanuatu

25,000 Bislama New Testaments. For the first time the New Testament is in the local language of the 96,000 inhabitants of the independent Island of Vanuatu in the South Pacific.

Region G — Europe

1. Denmark

A Bible reading plan for children. Main readings from the New Testament, and optional extra readings from the Old Testament. To be distributed through Christian youth organizations.

2. Greece

Ongoing translation work on the Good News New Testament in modern Greek. Greek Orthodox, Protestants, and Roman Catholics are all on the translations' team. Wide church support.

3. Switzerland (and other French speaking countries)

A braille Bible in French, for the blind. There are 458,637 blind Christians in the world who speak French — 4,422 in Switzerland — 22% of whom know Braille.

Region H — North America, Mexico, and Caribbean

1. Canada

A New Testament in the language of the Ojibwa Indians, who live on the border between Canada and the United States, near the Great Lakes.

2. Mexico

Five thousand popular-version Spanish Bibles for young people to give to their friends with whom they are sharing their faith — at work, in public places, churches, amusement parks, etc.

3. Jamaica

Scripture leaflets to back-up a national evangelistic crusade in Jamaica. 300,000 leaflets to be given away free.

Roles (optional)

Ten possible roles are suggested below for each region:

Region A — Latin America

A multinational executive — converted at last year's book fair
El Salvador liberation fighter
Bolivian peasant — unable to read
Christian Lord Mayor of El Salvador's third largest city
Missionary in Bolivia — used to serve in Argentina
Argentinian pastor
Bible Society General Secretary in Argentina
Literacy worker in Bolivia
American school teacher in El Salvador
Member of the British diplomatic staff in Argentina
Bible Society film projectionist in Bolivia
Founder of "Urban Operation"

Region B — The Muslim world

Egyptian student — converted through a Scripture selection
Bookshop manager in Algiers
Sunday-school teacher in Algiers
Pastor's wife in Egypt
Algerian politician — opposed to closed religious policy
Bible Society enthusiast in Turkey
Turkey businessman — converted at last year's Ankara trade fair
Literacy worker in Egypt
A worker on Bible Society stall at this year's Ismir fair
British businessman in Algiers — keen on evangelism

Region C — British Isles

Member of the committee of "Evangelism among housewives"
Evangelist among gypsies
Pastor of Welsh-speaking Baptist church
A Christian gypsy
Marketing manager of Bible Society with responsibility for Wales
Author of the housewives' Scripture selection
Ex-Jehovah's Witness
Translator of the Romany Gospels
English speaker in Wales
Trainer in door-to-door evangelism
Bible Society representative in Wales
Bible Society representative in Ireland

Region D — The communist world

Christian printer with experience of printing Christian literature in Chinese
Christian pastor in China
Christian businessman working short-term in China
A Christian from Armenia
Leader of the Baptist denomination in U.S.S.R.
A one-time Bible smuggler
Bible Society worker for Eastern Europe
Leader of Bible Society in Poland
Politician in Poland
Pastor in Poland

Region E — Central and Southern Africa

A refugee just returned to Zimbabwe
An English missionary in Rwanda
A Christian freedom-fighter in Zimbabwe
Bible Society employee in Sudan
Church member in Rwanda
Wife of Bible Society Secretary in Sudan
Literacy worker in Rwanda
Converted Muslim in Sudan
Member of the Government in Zimbabwe
A translator of the Kinyarwanda Bible

Region F — South East Asia

Pastor of a growing Indonesian church
Translator of the Bengali Muslim Bible
Indonesian Sunday-school teacher
Vanuatu political leader
Translator of the Bislama New Testament
Bible distributor in Bangladesh
United Nations' literacy worker in Indonesia
Missionary in Vanuatu
Evangelist among Muslim prisoners in Bangladesh
Prison visitor in Indonesia

Region G — Europe

Christian teacher of the blind in France
Christian scout leader in Denmark
Greek Orthodox Bible translator

Blind French person
Greek pastor
Politician in Denmark
Bible Society employee in Switzerland
Youth evangelist in Athens
Pastor in Denmark
Roman Catholic church leader in Greece

Region H — North America, Mexico, and Caribbean

A missionary among the Ojibwa Indians
Youth evangelist in Mexico City
Church leader in Jamaica
A translator of the popular version Spanish Bible
Specialist in the history of North American Indians
Ex Rastafarian in Kingston, Jamaica
Christian policeman in Mexico City
Mexican pastor
Translator of the Ojibwa New Testament
Coordinator of evangelistic crusade in Jamaica

Other uses

1. The same game-structure lends itself well to exploring international development issues. You could, for example, create up to twenty-four cards describing development projects — covering the full range of self-help, water provision, health care, famine relief, industrial investment, education, etc., which require roughly the same amount of money. With or without roles, the players must prioritize the projects, and present them to some (real or fictitious) international agency. This will easily raise key issues — for example is long-term self help more worthwhile than first-aid famine relief? Can we choose? It will be very simplified, as is the Bible Society game above, but it will be powerful.

2. Likewise, any current national issue which might give rise to "projects" can be inserted into this game structure. Unemployment is an example. Many projects exist to help the unemployed — community work, job creation, voluntary schemes, drop-in centres, counselling services, financial help, retraining, leisure facilities, etc.

Use your own knowledge or research to create up to twenty-four "project cards" that describe these responses to the problem of unemployment. Split the country into up to eight areas, allocating three projects to each area. Then, as above, propose them to a regional "unemployment authority", who then propose one project only to the national "Unemployment Planning Committee". They must select half the projects and reject the other half.

Designing your own games

—A conversation

Trevor: Well that's that. We've finished.

Jim: Enough there to last most groups a couple of years!

T: Except . . .

J: Except what?

T: Don't you think we ought to go further? Do something about designing your own games. If anyone's really got the game bug, that's what they'll want to do next.

J: That's true. But how can we do it? Everyone designs games differently. You and I, for instance. My approach to designing a game is very different from yours.

T: My problem is always getting started. Getting the ideas flowing in the first place. Whereas yours, you always say, is finishing. You're full of bright ideas but can't seem to pin them down.

J: Which is probably why we enjoy working together. So my number one rule for designing games would be to find someone to work with.

T: Yes. Someone you get on with, but if possible someone with a different kind of approach to you. Because in game design you need two sorts of people. A lateral-thinking type. The sort of person who says, "What would happen if we combined snakes and ladders, the book of Hosea, a pile of hymnbooks, and a trip to the fish and chip shop".

J: And then there needs to be someone who replies, "Nothing", or "The Hosea bit's good!"

T: Once you've found a partner, then you need to find a subject . . .

J: Not always . . .

T: No, not always.

J: Some of my best games have started from the other end. I've thought of a game model that would work, and then looked around for a subject it could help people learn about. The DIY Bible was like that. Having realized the potential of the model — creating lots of things, and then choosing from what has been created — I only then realized how like the process of Bible formation this was.

T: Yes, I agree. But we'll come back to that. It is much more likely that people will want to prepare a game on a given subject.

J: Because they've got a group to lead this weekend on the subject of "relationships", and need a game to use.

T: Exactly.

J: First thing is to check that no one else has done a game on the subject.

T: Saves some time. Look through any games books. And if you find one, use that. Or adapt it. There's not much point in spending hours of valuable time preparing a game only to discover you've invented exactly the same game as someone else.

J: It's happened to me a couple of times.

T: And there is another point. Starting on Monday to design a game for use on Saturday is far too late. You need more time than that. Try to think at least three weeks ahead.

J: So here we are. Three weeks away. We have a sympathetic collaborator. We have a group to lead on the subject of relationships, and we want a game on relationships. First we decide what aspect of relationships we are talking about.

T: Well, the group are older teens. About twenty of them. So it's about romances, dating, and sex . . .

J: What an easy subject we've chosen. Anything more specific?

T: In school, there is a lot of talk about the conquest aspect of relationships. People try to win the most physically attractive partner. Often one person feels left out, although they are probably really nice people.

J: Not just in school though, Trevor. That happens in church youth groups . . .

T: . . . church adult groups . . .

J: . . . and people get hurt. Yes. It's an important subject.

T: So let's try that. Let's focus on the fact that many groups treat relationships, particularly boy/girl ones, like a game which you win or lose. And maybe that is wrong.

J: Maybe?

T: Yes . . . only maybe. After all it's just a phase, and the point of the game in the first place is not to point to what's right or wrong, but to explore the consequences of how something *is*. That's what the introduction to this book was all about, remember? Games look at attitudes, behaviour, feelings, and consequences, not truth or doctrine.

J: Yes, teacher!

T: So having spotted a subject we look for a model that might work. We look at existing games. We brainstorm. Write down all the possibilities. We don't discuss them to start with. Then from the final list, choose two or three.

J: What have we got?

T: A bartering or swapping game, like "Little Bible" (page 28).

J: Could we have the men owning the women, and swapping them?

T: Are you joking? A game shouldn't reinforce undesirable behaviour.

J: How about a role-play? Each person takes the role of a Casanova, and they try to collect as many partners as possible . . .

T: . . . and everyone ends up rolling about in the youth club annex.

J: And the minister walks in . . .

T: And I have to explain . . . "We're learning about relationships" . . .

J: No! Take three. How about a role-reversal? Men become women, and vice-versa.

T: More promising.

J: And what are they trying to achieve?

T: Points. They earn points for how "valuable" the person they go out with on Saturday night is.

J: So the game lasts eight weeks?

T: No. Half-an-hour, but every five minutes we have a Saturday night!

J: I see.

T: And the players are each given a totally arbitrary "value".

J: This begins to sound remarkably like "Matching game".

T: Well, we did fix the conversation a bit. If people want to know the end of this story they can look at page 66 and see how the game turned out. But for now, let's see what we learn from this process.

J: Well, there's the importance of brainstorming. Every time you start anything it's best to write down as many possible solutions as you can. Don't discuss them. Just list them. Then come back to them at the end. Pick the three best. Then opt for one of those.

T: Then second, there is the importance of models. A game model is just a type of game. And, strange to say, in all the thousands of games that must have been invented, there really aren't that many models.

J: Let's list some models.

T: Card games. Like rummy.

J: Good for teaching facts. Collect a set of true statements about such-and-such, and discard false ones.

T: Role-play. We've said a lot about that in this book.

J: Yes. But we haven't touched on very simple role-plays. They can be the best way to learn about other people. Put yourself in their shoes. How do they feel? For example, before an evangelistic mission, how many churches dare get their members to role-play what it's like to be on the receiving end of a visit by someone from the church? If they did they might not be so shocked when people refuse to reply to the knock on the door.

T: How about board games? Board games are an excellent way to scale down and simplify real life. Like Monopoly simplifies the property market.

140

J: And Monopoly is also a good example of negotiation and barter. Or buying and selling. Lots of games use that. Like "Little Bible". Trying to trade something can help you see its value.

T: What else is there? Collecting information — a sort of guided treasure-hunt. Prioritizing — like "First things first".

J: Fantasy games — like "Dungeons and Dragons".

T: I'm not sure that's a good model to follow — a lot of people are suspicious of that. And really it's an extension of role-play, isn't it.

J: Computer games. They need a lot of setting up, but they can deal with complicated subjects . . .

T: Don't mention computers, please. I used to spend all day with them.

J: All right! Quiz games?

T: Well, they're not really simulation games are they? Their internal logic isn't terribly interesting. Get it right, win a tea set, get it wrong, win a weekend in Swindon!

J: Hey! You seem to be throwing out most of my suggestions at the moment.

T: Nothing personal, I promise you! I just don't think we are going to have enough space to list all possible game models.

J: But have you ever noticed how each of us returns to our favourite model? I can be pushing along thinking I've got a completely original game, and then all of sudden I realize it's only subtly different from the last one I worked on. So a lot of my games have a "prioritizing phase" during which players faced by a number of options have to put them in an order of priority and discard all but the top ones.

T: Yes. Game-makers *do* tend to re-invent the same game over and over again. What other important points are there?

J: Be practical. From your long list of possible subjects and models you will eliminate those that are boring, or require a budget of £10,000, or take three weeks to play. You will also remove those that are manipulative.

T: So now you are onto the next stage. You have a game idea. You must now go through it again and again, revising it, adapting it. Always being prepared to drop it if it appears not to be working. Almost all the games in this book were radically altered several times before they ever made it to the starting block. And there are many more games even now sitting in the filing cabinet, or burning on the Lambeth Council Rubbish tip. Anyway, what happens next?

J: Things we usually discuss together are . . .

T: Are the rules clear?

J: Is there a fairly obvious playing strategy?

T: But not too obvious! Are all players involved — not just those with a chance of winning?

J: Is the outcome variable enough?

T: Does it expect too much of people, or too little? If you've got all those things right, you should be on target.

J: And what are the most likely things to spoil a game?

T: I think the biggest mistake is to make a game too complex, because you want it to "be like life". With the result that it takes an hour to introduce. No one understands it. And no clear playing strategy emerges.

J: And the second big mistake is to "fix" a game. That's a great temptation when you use games for Christian purposes.

T: Yes. It's the temptation of power. You may have a very specific thing you wish the participants to learn, but you cannot fix it so that, and only that, can be learned. Of course, if a game is teaching facts that's more possible — TACADE produce a card game called "Alcohol — what do you know", that does just that, and very effectively, too.
But if the idea is to teach that one attitude is better than another, you'll come unstuck. Remember that game you once produced which was a battle between the Status-quos, the Get-up-and-gos, the I-don't-knows, and the Told-you-sos? It was a great idea but the mistake you made was to set out to show that a Get-up-and-go attitude was better than a Status-quo attitude. And of course the Status-quos could see how things were loaded against them, and didn't join in. If you try to fix a game, expect problems. What else?

J: I always spend time with the Bible, as well.

T: You would. It's your job.

J: No, I mean it. There are lots of problems associated with using the Bible in games.

T: We've explained that already.

J: I know. Which makes this stage all the more important. If the aim is to explore the Bible, then you must spend time reflecting on how the Bible might be relevant.

T: Like we did on "One-hundred-thousand pounds".

J: Exactly. For the first few plays, that had no overt biblical exploration at all. But having reflected on what biblical principles might be relevant, I persuaded you to put in that dotty clause in the old lady's will about spending the money in accordance with her favourite passage — Matthew 5.13–16. So now people have to reflect on the Bible.

T: Yes, it seems to work, as well. Which reminds me of another important general point. Don't assume that just because a game skates near a subject, that participants will fall in!

J: Can you explain that a bit more?

T: Yes. Once a game starts, players will usually take the quickest possible route to completing the task. So if the success of the game depends on the

players actually doing something which is incidental or "bypassable", you can bet the game will flop.

J: For example?

T: I mentioned in "Mix'n'match" that clever-clogses should not just cut up a photocopied passage, because if you do the players will quickly rush to fit the passage together along the lines. You might fondly dream that the players are so keen on the Bible that they will read the passage to check they are correct, but it's very unlikely. So if you want something, anything, to be considered in the game, then you need to make it essential to completing the task. So in "Mix'n'match" they have to *read and understand* the passage. It's all they have to go on.

J: Right, let's go on ourselves. Now for the exciting bit. Test, test, test. Some games are dead simple — indeed you may have missed out all the phases we've mentioned so far — but you can't miss out this one. Every game needs all the testing you can give it. After the first time it probably won't change that much, but each time out you will do a little more fine-tuning. Start off by testing it with your own group.

T: Yes. The first time out is always a bit nerve-racking. But it's helpful to remember that the players probably want it to succeed as much as you do. Especially if you have told them they are guinea-pigs. You can modify your game during its first play. Or replay it immediately after with modified rules.

J: That sounds awful.

T: I know. But with the players on your side it can actually work very well.

J: And the debriefing?

T: Difficult first time. You can spend so much time talking about the game that you fail to discover what people learned about the subject, and issues raised by the game. So make sure you have planned your questions well. And cover both the game itself, and the subject.

J: Then, after three weeks work you just dump it?

T: Often. That's why we bothered to say at the start of the book that you have to be committed to this way of learning to think it worth designing your own games. You invest a lot of time.

J: But then you might be able to try it out with other groups. And if you do, you must have done a thorough evaluation of what happened when you played it with your group. An honest evaluation. Did it work? Will it always work?

T: So that's that.

J: Almost. You told me I could finish with my hobby-horse.

T: Linear and lateral.

J: That's it. We've talked as if game design goes A, B, C . . . I don't think it usually does. It more often goes Q, Z, @, *, ¼, %%%, and then crash, you suddenly realize you have a good idea. It's the lateral thinking that comes first. The linear that comes next. So the most important tool for the game designer is a note-book. To collect those little gems of inspiration that suddenly flash through the mind, in the bath, on the bus, in a dream . . .

T: So as Jim disappears into his reverie, it's left to me to encourage you to invent and try out your own games. And to try to put together a conclusion . . .

Conclusion

If you've tried any of the games in this book you should by now be convinced of their value. If you've tried them all then you're lucky to still have energy to open this book!

But what's in this book is only a beginning. We hope that you will use the resources listed on page 148 to help fill in some of the gaps in this book.

We have only touched on the theoretical side of games. You could spend many fruitful hours reading the experts on the subjects.

Nor have we included any of the excellent drama/role-play exercises which allow you to experience the agony of the children of Israel, or the courage of Moses. We have omitted such games in favour of ones that are planted firmly in the twentieth century.

We have deliberately concentrated most on those games that seem to fit in some ways the interests and inclinations of the church groups, and especially youth groups that we have known.

It will be clear that we believe games are a valuable contribution to the life of any group. So let's finish with a question.

If games are so valuable, how has the church managed so long without them?

You see the problem. If games are necessary, how could the church have managed without them up till now? If they are not necessary, why start tinkering with experimental ideas at this crucial time in its history?

A good question of course, and one which could equally well be applied to film-strips, videos, and rock-music, but not to Christian drama which started at least a thousand years ago.

Although it's part of the answer, it's not enough just to say that the church must use today's methods, because we all know that there are *some* of today's methods which we wouldn't touch with a barge-pole.

It's more than that. We think there are two parts to the answer. First, people today are educated not to accept facts on authority. Instead they are encouraged to find out for themselves, even about issues which are tangential to their daily lives.

For example, a child learning history will expect to clamber over castles, to touch armour, to make a model of Stonehenge, to make a record of graveyards, to tape-record reminiscences and so on. And the same in science lessons — there they will have a chance to do experiments which twenty-five years ago would not have been seen outside a University laboratory.

The same seems true of us adults. Television has taught us to expect evidence for everything. Even an earthquake or a famine doesn't seem quite real until we've experienced the effects on television, and felt some genuine emotion.

And museums are changing from places of authoritative silence into

Aladdin's caves of experience. You push buttons, hear sounds, smell smells, and all this to help you feel what it was like to be there.

This means that the church may have to pick up new techniques to meet what is a new need. To learn by experience, rather than listen to someone in authority.

The final part of the answer might relate to the way we live. Gone are the small communities, changing slowly, relatively close to the countryside, where each person had their part to play; where a death was a big event; where songs and stories were shared, and the traveller was welcome for his tales.

Instead there is the high-rise block and the ever-present television in the living room. And a world of change.

The same is true of churches. Very few people now worship at the same church all their lives. So the depth of knowledge and shared experience of each other in a church has only a short time to grow, and does not have the richness which comes from a life-time together.

So perhaps games might go a small way to filling the gap in the way we live now. And if they can bring people closer together to explore, and to see the richness of the world God has given us, then . . . everyone's a winner.

Which game Index

The following table will help show you at a glance what kind of groups each game is most suitable for and how long they will take you to prepare and play. In the "Suitable for" columns ■ means the game is well-suited to such a group, while □ means it could be used with care and/or adaptation with such a group.

	Suitable for:										Likely preparation time:			Playing time (including debriefing):		
	Ages under 15	Ages 15–19	Young adults over 19	General adults	Newcomers to games	Groups sized less than 20	Groups sized 21–40	Groups sized more than 40	Minimal interest in Christianity	Great interest in Christianity	Under 1 hour	1–2 hours	Over 2 hours	Under 1 hour	1–2 hours	Over 2 hours
Section A																
Little Bible (page 28)		■	■	■	■	□	■	□		■	■			■		
Connections (page 32)	■				■	■	■	□		■		■		■		
DIY Bible (page 37)		■	■	□	■	□	■	■		■					■	■
Best seller (page 49)		■	■		■	■	□	□		■				■		■
Mix'n'match (page 54)	□	■	■	■	■	■	■	■				■			■	
Give us a proverb (page 57)	■	□			■	■	■	■	■	□		■			■	
Section B																
Matching game (page 66)		■	■			■	■		■			■			■	
Money, money, money (page 77)		■	■	■	□	■	■	■	■	■				■		■
Bits and pieces (page 89)		□	■	■		■	□			■				■	■	
One-hundred-thousand pounds (page 95)	□	■	■	■	□			■	□	□	■	■			■	
Roll out the barrel (page 101)		□	■	■		■	■	■	■					■		■
Zac's map (page 122)	□	■	□		■	■	■		□	■	■				■	
First things first (page 126)		■	■	■			■	■				■			■	

Resources for games

There are literally hundreds of organizations that have developed games and simulations for use in their own training. There are also many books that investigate the theory and practice of gaming in depth.

SAGSET has produced a comprehensive bibliography of books and games.
You can contact them at:
SAGSET
Dept. of Extra Mural Studies
Loughborough University of Technology
LOUGHBOROUGH
Leics.
LE11 3TU

Other organizations that publish games we have found useful in churches are:

Christian Aid, 240–250 Ferndale Rd, LONDON, SW9 8BH

Cockpit Arts workshop, Gateforth Street, LONDON, NW8 8EH

Oxfam, 274 Banbury Rd, OXFORD, OX2 7JF

TACADE, 3rd Floor, Furness House, Trafford Rd, SALFORD, Lancs, M5 2XJ

Books that we would recommend, either as a source of warm-ups or of other game models, are:

Bob Moffett, *Crowd-breakers* (Pickering and Inglis, 1983)
Bob Moffett, *Crowd-makers* (Pickering and Inglis, 1985)
Donna Brandes and Howard Phillips, *Gamester's Handbook No. 1* (Hutchinson Educational 1979)
Donna Brandes, *Gamester's Handbook No. 2* (Hutchinson Educational, 1984)
Matt Weinstein and Joel Goodman, *Playfair* (Impact Publishers, 1978)
Published in U.S.A. Available in U.K. through the New Games Foundation.
McMullen, *Winners all – Cooperative Games for all ages* (Pax Christi, 1980)
M R Goodlad and E Whitton, *Eight Games for Group Leaders* (Methodist Church Division of Education and Youth, 1981)
Available direct from the publishers at 2 Chester House, Pages Lane, LONDON, N10 1PR

Index of Bible references

This index includes all the Bible passages and verses mentioned in this book.

		page
Genesis	1.1–2	33
Genesis	2.7	33
Genesis	2.18–25	76
Genesis	6.13–22	33
Genesis	19	7
Exodus	3.4–6	33
Exodus	12.21–28	33
Exodus	12.25–27	7
Exodus	20.13–16	33
Exodus	22.28	33
Exodus	26.31–33	33
Leviticus	14.1–32	33
Deuteronomy	8.3	33
Joshua	1.9	33
Ruth	4.18–22	33
1 Samuel	3.20	33
1 Samuel	21.1–6	33
2 Samuel	12.1–15	7
1 Kings	10.4–7	33
2 Kings	1.9–16	33
2 Kings	2.1–18	33
2 Kings	5.1–14	33
2 Chronicles	24.1–14	81
Job	5.13	33
Psalm	14.1–3	33
Psalm	104.15	111
Proverbs	1.3	57
Proverbs	1.1–6	60
Proverbs	3.29–35	109
Proverbs	10.10	58
Proverbs	11.22	60
Proverbs	14.26	58
Proverbs	15.13	58
Proverbs	16.11	58
Proverbs	16.12	58
Proverbs	17.1	58
Proverbs	17.9	58
Proverbs	17.12	60
Proverbs	19.3	58
Proverbs	19.11	58
Proverbs	19.17	58
Proverbs	20.1	58,111
Proverbs	20.19	58
Proverbs	20.21	58
Proverbs	21.9	58
Proverbs	23.29–35	109
Proverbs	25.20	58
Proverbs	26.15	58
Proverbs	27.20	58

		page
Proverbs	29.17	58
Proverbs	30.8–9	77,83
Proverbs	30.18–19	58
Proverbs	31.30	58
Ecclesiastes	5.10–12	83
Isaiah	61.1–2	33
Ezekiel	32.7	33
Daniel	9.27	33
Micah	5.2	33
Matthew	2.6	33
Matthew	5.13–16	75,97
Matthew	6.24–34	84,87
Matthew	6.28–30	33
Matthew	10.5–10	85
Matthew	13.31	97
Matthew	17.27	7
Matthew	19.16–22	33
Matthew	19.16–30	82
Matthew	21.12–17	87
Matthew	24.15	33
Matthew	24.29	33
Matthew	25.42–45	97
Mark	2.23–28	33
Mark	12.13–17	87
Mark	14.66–72	33
Luke	3.4–6	47
Luke	4.4	33
Luke	4.16–21	33
Luke	4.25–27	33
Luke	5.14	33
Luke	9.18–20	33
Luke	9.54	33
Luke	10.1–20	7
Luke	12.32–34	85
Luke	18.18–30	122
Luke	19.1–10	124
Luke	21.1–4	87
Luke	23.45	33
Luke	24.50–53	33
John	7.37–38	33
John	12.2–8	97
John	13.1	33
John	13.1–9	75
John	21.6	7
Acts	2.43–45	85
Acts	2.16–21	47
Acts	13.20	33
Acts	17.16	33
Acts	23.5	33

		page
Romans	3.10–12	33
Romans	3.10–18	47
Romans	8.1–30	54
Romans	12.1–13	75
Romans	14	109
1 Corinthians	3.19	33
1 Corinthians	8 and 10	109
1 Corinthians	14.1–25	54
1 Corinthians	15.1–58	6

		page
Ephesians	2.19–22	89,91
Ephesians	5.18	111
Philippians	3.1–21	54
1 Timothy	2.13	33
1 Timothy	3.8	111
Hebrews	5.11—6.12	54
Hebrews	11.7	33
James	2.14–26	54

150

General Index

This is not a comprehensive index. It simply lists some of the issues that have most concerned us in this book, and points you towards the games or the pages where that issue is most fully explored.

	page
Bible	
problems of using it in games	6
distance between our world and it	66/67
reaching a balanced viewpoint	108
proof texts	121
valuing it	28, 126ff
Old and New Testament	32
forming the canon	37ff
designing an appropriate cover to express its message	49ff
reading it out loud	54ff
proverbs	57ff
relationships	66ff
teaching on money	77ff
teaching on the church	89ff
alcohol	101ff
Jesus' priorities	122ff
Blockers	127, 128
Briefing	14
Competition	1
Debriefing	
general	20–25
trouble-shooting	23–25

	page
Definitions	4
Designing games	138ff
Game models	
general	139, 141
raising an issue	66
role-playing interview	77ff
meeting games	102
Groups – how to form them	41
Information input	80
Leadership style	15–16
Phrasing questions	23, 24
Preparation	14
Role-cards	110
Role-play	107
Rules	4
Testing	143
Time-limits	13
Voting	99
Warming up	17–19

Other creative resources from Bible Society

Picture It!
by Paul Clowney

Packed full of ideas on how you can use your artistic skills and interests to serve God and his church. Written by artist, designer, and teacher Paul Clowney, specifically to help encourage a wider use of the visual arts in the church.

Using the Bible in Drama
by Steve and Janet Stickley and Jim Belben

Now established as a standard work on the subject of starting a church drama group. It presents for free performance some of Footprints Theatre Company's most famous sketches, and also includes advice on warming up, studying the Bible, writing through improvisation, performing, and presenting your sketches.

Move Yourselves
By Gordon and Ronni Lamont

Eleven movement, mime, and dance workshops. Including four original performance pieces for the church festivals of Christmas, Easter, Pentecost, and Harvest. Written out of the vast workshop experience of the leaders and founders of Kinetik Theatre, Gordon and Ronni Lamont.

Show Me!
by Judy Gattis Smith

Fifteen techniques – and thirty ready-to-use examples – revealing how to use drama with children aged 3–13. Written by a Director of Christian Education in a church in Williamsburg, Virginia, U.S.A., then tested, revised and republished for use in the U.K.

Jim Belben and Trevor Cooper, authors of *Everyone's a Winner*, would like to know how you get on with these games. They would also be interested to hear of any game *you* develop as a result of using this book.
You can write to them at the following address:

Jim Belben and Trevor Cooper
c/o Bible Society
Stonehill Green
Westlea
Swindon SN5 7DG
Wilts